A Mongolian Memoir

D0875061

Diane M. Height

All Photographs by Diane M. Height

Author Photo by Roger Mullenhour

ISBN (paperback) 979-8-9874192-0-5
ISBN (ebook): 979-8-9874192-1-2

Cover and book design by Mayfly Design

Library of Congress Catalog Number: 2022922752

To Aunt Marye and Grandmom with love.
I would not be the person I am today
without your adventurous spirits.

"In out-of-the-way places of the heart,
Where your thoughts never think to wander,
This beginning has been quietly forming,
Waiting until you were ready to emerge."

— John Donahue, *For A New Beginning*

Contents

Dear Reader,

I wrote *A Mongolian Memoir* to share my experiences living and teaching in Mongolia at a crossroads in my life that some might consider the beginning of their "third act."

I hope my story will inspire others to realize they can "reach for the stars" at any age.

Please join me as I recall and reflect on each moment in time.

Diane M. Height

CHAPTER 1

Freedom

"I only went out for a walk . . . "

— John Muir

I was only going to Mongolia to teach for two years. Little did I know the experience would seep into my bones, into the marrow of who I really was, and change me forever so that when I finally did come home . . . I was not home.

I felt as though my soul found what it had been searching for . . . in this place of *gers* and Chinggis Khan, in this adventure. Call it wanderlust, tag it with whatever name you chose, but my true safe haven was the adventure, another place. My North Star.

My soul soared like an eagle, daring to be free.

I talked to other expats about this wanderlust, this adventure; and I never needed to finish the thought or words; they knew what I was talking about . . . the connection was there.

But it was also more—it was Mongolia.

People here ask if I will return.

Even today, I would go back in a flash!

CHAPTER 2

Leaving

The moon had always fascinated me. I wasn't sure why, though I knew I was in good company. How could we not be mesmerized by something so imperfectly perfect and shining so brightly against the darkness? In my own case, I thought it was always a promise of hope.

The moon in Mongolia especially . . . it seemed to creep up over the hills behind my apartment, like a cat that meant me well, but still wanted to be stealthy. As I laid in bed, watching the beginnings—a soft glow that got more pronounced as it finally crested on the hilltop promising the child in me that peace, that hope.

As a child, I watched it from my bedroom window as it rose. For a long time, I didn't realize that the moon's glow seeping through the screen's mesh was why I always saw a cross. I thought it was a sign from God; and why not? Every night I went to bed waiting for that sign, especially when the house was filled with sadness. Angry words from my parents' bedroom filled my ears even when I tried to block them out. It wasn't only words that conveyed light as well as darkness— feelings and thoughts, good and bad, moved across time and space and knew no boundaries. This is a story told many times; but when it's your story, it's somehow different.

I was divorcing. And for the second time. This time was different, as I'm sure they always are. We had fewer arguments, but I learned that wasn't always good. Silence can be a terrible thing. I had seen, and yet I was to learn in the world I was heading toward, that silence, a vastness, a wonder, can be a beautiful thing too.

Our whole lives, we heard, "What doesn't kill you makes you stronger." Sometimes it was hard to tell whether life was killing me or making me stronger. I also heard, "You'll get passed the divorce; you'll flourish; something else is out there for you."

Didn't I know all of this? But at two o'clock in the morning, the demons had their own playbook, and they were anything but dumb.

Here I was waiting in the wee hours of the morning for the shuttle that would take me, three rather large suitcases, and three carry-ons to LAX, and then on to my final destination: Ulaanbaatar, the capital of Mongolia. I was going to be a teacher again, but this time at an international school in Asia. I was excited, but I was definitely scared.

I knew I was embarking on something I kept hidden for years—a part of me I had denied or was afraid to talk about or even think about.

If you let good come in, will it stay? Or will it taunt you with its allure and then vanish?

But other words came as the plane doors closed, "You will find the life that has been waiting for you."

My own thoughts were still more persistent, *Is it necessary to travel so far to find peace and hope?*

Were these the demons or something else?

Hadn't I always wanted to live and work in a foreign country as if I was Isak Dinesen crossing the Serengeti. She with wild animals, disease, unknown encounters.

But looking back on what I did in foreign places since I first started—living in extreme temperatures, dealing with political unrest, COVID-19. Had I not become a type of Isak Dinesen in *Out of Africa*? An adventuress, a wanderer.

Had I finally let the good stay?

Mongolia began for me as a hope to help me leave what failed to make me as happy as I wanted to be; and when I reached it and stayed there, that hope grew . . . as I did.

———

How hard it is to escape from places. However carefully one goes, they hold you–you leave bits of yourself fluttering on the fences–little rags and shreds of your very life.

— Katherine Mansfield

CHAPTER 3

Motorcycle Guy

Motorcycle Guy in the Gobi Desert

My girlfriend and I were traveling in the Gobi Desert of Mongolia—that vast, seemingly barren land that went on forever and only shared a southern border with China. A few Bactrian, two-humped camels, were off in the distance. The largest population of Bactrian camels in the world were here. We had a Mongolian driver, Bata, who spoke no English, and Soko, our tour guide, who spoke excellent English, a fair amount of German, and was an excellent cook. But we were still two Americans alone, feeling like kids pretending to know what they were doing.

I'd been to the Gobi twice over the five years I lived in the capital city of Ulaanbaatar, or UB, as the locals called it, and now I am teaching English at an international school. I had always been challenged with learning foreign languages. In fact, every time I went to a new foreign country, a good friend teased me about "learning" the language. He, on the other hand, had no problem; but "I have some kind of block," I said, and we'd have a good laugh.

But I did learn rather well (I was definitely proud of myself) the correct way to pronounce Ulaanbaatar, which began with the *oo* sound, as in "who."

The 1,200-mile round trip from UB was six days and five nights in a 4WD. We stayed in the Mongolian nomadic *gers*—the traditional round-shaped dwelling usually covered with a felt. I could see no roads in the desert, only bumpy dirt tracks. But even so, our driver seemed to know where he was going. Like a mirage, another vehicle appeared, and both drivers stopped long enough for a smoke.

I spotted him long before we stopped, a flash of water on the desert I wanted to be real. Any human being was like water in this desert. But wasn't he just a guy? A guy on a motorcycle, wearing the traditional Mongolian *deel* to keep warm, and black laced boots, but not the typical Mongolian boots with the toes turned up to protect the earth. A baseball cap with the words "casual fashion" written across the front partially hid his face, along with the cellphone he had cradled in his hand. The more I stared, the more I envisioned him stepping out of a romance novel; his shaggy, black hair fell across his dark, brown skin. Why I didn't want to think I found him attractive, I didn't know. Independence, self-sufficiency. Silly as it sounded—something whispered "no" to anything that meant stopping, attaching, giving someone else the power. He reminded me of those bad boys from my youth, with their cocky attitude that said they could have anyone they wanted. The ones I thought I was no longer attracted to . . . even when they scared me. Maybe it was fear then, fear of the bad girl in me. I still didn't know.

How was it that my past seemed to creep in 6,100 miles from home? The ghosts of past—were they still with me?

I felt I had no choice but to move closer, telling myself I wanted a better shot. Usually I asked permission, not wanting to be disrespectful, but this time I raised my camera and clicked away. He was busy on his phone.

I went over to where my friend and Soko were standing.

"They use motorcycles to herd the camels. No big deal. Easier to get around," she said.

I caught her eyes as she spoke, and maybe it was my imagination but she seemed to smirk, her lips a tiny snake.

I turned to get back into the jeep and, as we drove away like a witch moth to the moon, I glanced one more time, wondering what I wanted to see.

CHAPTER 4

Gobi Desert

Gobi Desert at Sunset

Living in Mongolia for five years changed everything: how I lived and how I saw myself. there and also when I came home. I've always been open to change, and when I was there, I moved with an ease that even now after being "home" for several years, I seemed to have lost. I could still feel it trying to bubble up to the surface like air that could keep me alive— eyes young again with energy and a dream. Did I know this would happen to me? Was I happy that it had? Yes and no, like a double-edged sword.

At this point in my life, at age sixty-three, I was beginning to understand what it meant "to stay in the light," to listen to my heart, and follow the dream. But still at times, I was afraid to run my own race, caught up in the opinions of others.

Very few places in the world were as remote and barren as the Gobi Desert in southern Mongolia. This was my second time in the Gobi and my first time venturing out into Mongolia on my own with just a driver, Bayra, who spoke no English, and Ogi, my tour guide. Ogi knew a lot of English and was an excellent cook. Once again, I was traveling by 4WD and staying in the Mongolian nomadic gers.

I'd seen the most beautiful skies in the Mongolian countryside—stars that covered the blackness like a blanket protecting its ward, a full moon that was so big I thought maybe I could see ET riding across or Neil Armstrong's footprints. But on this night, outhouses were silhouetted against a fiery sky offering a somewhat mixed bag of comfort and fear. Not for the fainthearted. Wolves were around; we heard them howling sometimes late at night. Dogs wandered freely, partly to keep the wolves at bay and partly because the Mongolians didn't leash their dogs; they were work dogs, not pets. Not like the pets we had at home where we spent as much money keeping them healthy as we would another member of the family.

At 2:00 a.m. with flashlight in hand, I walked toward the outhouses. Two glowing red eyes approached. A dog. No growling, no teeth bared, but still my heart was pounding. I took a deep breath, realizing the dog was sniffing me. And somehow in that moment, I trusted the dog I didn't know, but I believed (or maybe wanted to believe it would keep me safe from the wolves).

I kept walking.

For obvious reasons, the outhouses weren't close to the

gers, and we were supposed to use them even though they were hard enough to maneuver during the day with figuring out the door and straddling two slates. And where was the TP? I tried not to think beyond that, deciding behind the gers was good enough for nighttime.

The sunset ended on the other side when it met the moon that seemed to grab the reds, gold, and even the blackness and swirled them around until they were engulfed in the bright, white light that hung right above the horizon. That moon that had always been my beacon . . . my hope and peace.

I'd never known whether I was a city girl or country girl; I thought both as I looked out at the vastness—incomprehensible—both of the land and of the sky. And I loved it! I offered up a silent prayer of thanks. I asked myself if this magic only happened here where time seemed to stop, so different from my world at home.

During my second year, my massage therapist said, "You like it here. I think you've become Mongolian."

I laughed but felt proud by her words—that feeling of belonging. Being a geographer, I knew how important "place" is: finding where you belong. I found a saying, "Never underestimate the pull of place. Find your place, and it will nurture you."

It seemed that I had always been searching to belong. Starting over, beginning again. A friend once told me, "You've reinvented yourself so many times."

I now know, that was a good thing for me. I always tried to push myself, to not be afraid to try. Even though trying at times could be trying, even for me.

After lowering my camera, I walked silently, as did the dog, in the darkness. I was going home permanently in a few months and, to what, I wasn't sure. I was still pulled by words like *shoulda, coulda* . . . and not always from others.

Tapes played in my head. I knew not to listen, but demons can be relentless.

Was it the place that opened the traveler, or the traveler who opened because she was traveling to that place?

No matter what, I had become Mongolian. I had changed forever, and I liked it.

CHAPTER 5

Tsagaan Sar

Tsagaan Sar at Sunrise

Some mysteries we thought we understood if we just tried, but they were beyond us and left to another time and place.

My second-grade teaching partner, Christy, her husband Steve, and I decided to get up at 4:00 a.m. along with other expats and Mongolians to make our way by bus out to the countryside about an hour from UB to the 130-feet Chinggis Khan statue to observe the very important holiday of Tsagaan Sar, the Mongolian Lunar New Year.

Tsagaan Sar meant literally "white moon."

Chinggis Khan Statue at Tsagaan Sar

The celebration was sort of like our American Thanksgiving with lots of food and lots of people, except celebrated in February. Businesses closed sometimes for several days. Men, women, and children dressed up in their traditional *deels* with elaborate headdresses for the girls and hats for the men. A *deel* is similar to a caftan or a tunic and usually worn with a sash, a great way to keep warm.

Cooking went on for weeks with women making the traditional *buuz*, the dumpling stuffed with beef, but many times made with mutton (not lamb) and cabbage.

At the end of my five years, my assistant, Muugii, invited me to her home to show me how to make buuz. She, of course, had been making it for a long time, starting out as a child tied to her mother's apron strings. Her young daughter joined us, and I took videos and then gave it a try. We all had a good laugh as I became covered in flour! But after returning home and during the holidays, I made it for my family. They were gracious, and it wasn't bad; but it wasn't Muugii's.

I was so impressed with the Mongolian people and their sense of family, solidarity, and extreme resiliency against all odds. I loved the holidays starting with Halloween right through New Year's. I was very family oriented, so I fit right in with the Mongolian people. Once they got to know you, you became part of them, part of the family, especially if you were older. They respected their elders and felt a sense of continuity with them.

During Tsagaan Sar, homes were open to family and friends, as people made their way around town and sometimes out into the countryside. Over the years, I was invited to various homes to help celebrate, which was an honor.

And so on that special day, we waited for the sunrise to welcome the new year. We started inside the building, but knew we had to venture outside to partake of the festivities. Because it was February, the temperature was very cold, around minus 30F. The three of us hated the cold; but there we were, bundled up, our hands freezing from trying to take pictures without gloves on. Even after five years, I could never keep my hands warm despite using two layers of gloves and every kind of material. It was a joke with those back home.

I was tempted to go back inside to the warmth, but then I saw her. She was walking alone along the well-worn snow path. She was dressed warmly wearing her deeI, but still she was walking away from the warmth of the building, further into the cold. Everything, including her and the snow, had an eerie blue cast as though some magic was about to happen.

And I knew I wanted it to be true.

I sensed her courage along with something else I couldn't explain, or didn't want to admit.

Just as a child growing up in New Jersey, when my dad drove my mother, brother, and me through the woods, I sought magic. I wanted those woods to go on forever, to never end, with mythical creatures living in the dark forest, hidden from all eyes except mine.

I remember thinking I wasn't afraid. Fantasy had always been a comfort.

I made up stories, even repeated them aloud as my dad drove. My eyes never left the trees until the trees left me craning my neck for one last glimpse. I wanted to lose myself in the mystery.

One of my favorite stories was the Russian folk tale, *Peter and the Wolf.* The forest deep and empty, the unknown, even the fear. It all held me in its grip!

I looked back at the Chinggis Khan statue made of stainless steel, shining brightly even in the darkness, strong and powerful like the Khan must have been.

As the sky became alive, a drummer beat rhythmically, announcing the new year. Some chanted. A woman standing near me was offering biscuits, candy, fruit, and milk for peace, prosperity, and blessings for family and friends. I hoped the gods were hungry.

When we first arrived, we were given very tiny pieces of wood and, according to our birth year, we had to walk in certain places around the statue, distributing the wood and offering blessings. I only got so far in my walk because the freezing cold was unforgiving.

As the sun rose higher, the drummer beat louder, and the lone woman kept walking. The eerie blue was replaced by a pinkish hue.

I glanced at the Khan, envisioning the horse and rider leaping off the building and riding away. Would he take her with him? Could he take me? Would I go?

I watched her walk.

We had to hurry inside, because they had prepared a feast that included slices of sheep to be distributed to all: not your typical American breakfast, but good to keep the body fueled and warm.

When we went outside to leave, I looked for her, but she was gone. I stopped to stare, imagining she made her way to the end then vanished. Maybe on a dragon. Was she the keeper of the white moon? Perhaps a traveler from another time? Or did she leave with him?

For a moment, that little girl from New Jersey was standing to board the bus and again wondering if she would go.

CHAPTER 6

Bactrian Camels

Bactrian Camels

The cerulean blue sky met the golden grassland fields as if an artist's brush had painted the scene.

And why not?

Wispy clouds barely visible added to the background, not the usual angry ones you see in Mongolia that promise to take your breath away.

Was something else going on?

As we made our way across the open land, they appeared on the horizon like a ghost train. We stopped to watch. I imagined we were more curious about them than they were about us. Almost as one, they moved closer like soldiers preparing for battle.

But I wasn't afraid.

In the five years I lived in Mongolia, I discovered this land held many secrets . . . some to be discovered and some forever hidden like mysteries not meant to harm us, but in their own way made us better.

It seemed there was always a struggle between the land and its people. They called it fate, destiny—the great Khan's spirit always present.

I asked myself, "Where is their herder?" I thought the leader looked over at me and if he could talk would say they had done this trek many times; it was in their genes and they didn't need the likes of us.

They seemed aloof, but wasn't that what we always said about camels? Aiming my camera, I moved a little closer carefully. Without breaking stride, they moved away ever so slightly again as though they were one. And who could say they weren't?

They were the Bactrian camels with two humps only found in the Gobi Desert of Mongolia and China. I traveled before into the Gobi Desert and had ridden them. Safer I felt than the Mongolian horses. But now I was an observer.

The driver turned off the engine, and we watched in silence as they moved across the desert, heads held high, almost like ballerinas ready to perform a plie or pirouette.

When I was young, I was a ballerina, and maybe I was thinking of those movements where I held my head up high, lost to the dance, to the music, as if nothing else existed. As though I didn't want anything else to exist but that moment. Any lingering pain that could be all-consuming was gone. Only the dance mattered.

Slowly we watched them disappear back into the painting. Lost in my own thoughts, I wondered if they were ever there, like so many mirages.

I remembered another time in the Ngorongoro Crater in Africa in a 4WD surrounded by lions, not camels.

Living in Mongolia always felt like living up in the air . . . as if you were with the gods.

CHAPTER 7

Caught in the Ice

Falling in the Ice in Northeastern Mongolia

I loved UB, but to get a feel for Mongolia you had to venture out of the city into the countryside. For me it meant staying in gers and not merely the upscale en suite ones with bathrooms attached, but living with families, living the way they lived. No running water. Instead outhouses or the nearest ground. No heating except by the stove, which I discovered wasn't fueled after 2:00 a.m. At 3:00 a.m. you make a serious decision about leaving whatever warmth there was left to relieve yourself. No showers. Pretty much the same clothes for a week.

But the tradeoff was the most beautiful country with nothing except a scattering of gers for miles on end. Spectacular sunsets and sunrises that you swear light the sky on fire by the hands of gods. The moon so big that you are sure you could reach out and take it for a ride. The warmth and hospitality of the people who, even though you don't speak each other's language, spoke a language beyond words. Fearsome horses. Bactrian camels. Crystal clear lakes. Sands that called to you like lost children. Did they know they were lost? Did they care? Why was it we cared so much? Why did I care so much? But I did. I always had, with parents, children, husbands, friends . . . sometimes to my own detriment, but I was learning. Mongolia was my classroom.

There I was not in the middle of blue oceans, but seas of yellow grasses. Chinggis Khan everywhere. Weathered faces of the old. Young children who cared for the goats as though they were the ones in charge, and who was I to say they were not?

I have been blessed to have traveled to some remote and beautiful places in my life, which made me wonder why I sometimes put up with the traffic and congestion of large metropolitan areas when I return to Southern California. Another story.

I didn't come by this ger thing easily. November break was coming up, and it would be a good time to travel—still cold mainly at night, but not the minus 40F that started in December and lasted for a solid three months!

A friend and I decided to venture into the northeastern part of Mongolia for almost a week, ending up near the Russian border. I booked with a local tour company/guide and was asked if I wanted to stay in gers the entire time or tourist hotels. I opted for one or two nights in a ger with the remainder in tourist hotels.

What was I thinking? Novice that I was, I thought the bathroom facilities would be better in the tourist hotels. Wrong! They were actually worse. Like the gers, there were no en suite bathrooms; but unlike the gers, it was hard to find privacy right outside the "hotels." More traffic, more people roaming around. I made do and put aside my "Western ways" and squatted as best as I could, with other gals not far away.

When I left Southern California for Mongolia to teach for two years, some of my friends and family questioned my choice. "Why Mongolia?" I heard over and over again.

A single older female in a developing country that few people in the US knew about or even where it was located. Some got confused and thought it was that small country in Europe that started with "*M*." They couldn't imagine me being where there wasn't an ocean or a Nordstrom.

But I wanted a place completely different from what I knew, and (in some cases) where I had traveled. My answer, even to this day, has always been, "Mongolia chose me."

We headed to Northeastern Mongolia, where heaven and earth fused into one part—a blank slate of blue sky colliding with an equally empty sea of yellow grass. Let your imagination wander to the scenery from *Dances with Wolves*. Besides the grasslands, the major feature of the region was the Khan Khentii Mountains. The area stretched from northeast of Ulaanbaatar to the Russian border and was the homeland of Chinggis Khan, ruler of Mongolia in 1206, and considered by many one of the greatest military leaders in history. At one time the Mongol Empire covered most of Asia and extended into Europe to the gates of Vienna. Chinggis Khan is still revered throughout Mongolia in every aspect of life. Something I didn't understand when I first arrived. Like a lot of Westerners, I was taught only the negative aspects of the Khan.

The trip was a five-day, four-night tour from UB to the northeastern corner of Mongolia, about twenty miles south of the Russian border, close to Siberia. Along the way, we stopped at the Baldan Baraivan Monastery and were captivated by the caretaker whose dark, etched-lined face was full of expression as he shared stories with our driver and tour guide. At one time, 3,000–8,000 Buddhists monks lived in the monastery, but it was destroyed by the Russians in the 1930s.

We drove the 1,000-mile round trip in a Russian minibus, I think one of the most durable vehicles ever made, and my first time. We had a Mongolian driver, Mugii ,and a tour guide, Bagii, who was another creative cook. They both spoke English.

The rivers at this time of the year were frozen over with ice, which meant if Mugii could drive across the ice and see some areas not usually accessible.

We were excited, my friend and I, since we like adventure!

The first time we came to a frozen river, about thirty feet wide, Mugii got out to test the ice to see if it could take the weight of the minibus with us in it. The next time, he had us get out of the vehicle and carefully, with the help of Bagii, walk across the ice.

I was not a daredevil when it came to extreme sports or vacations, but I was adventurous, having traveled to Africa numerous times, and once having an encounter with a lion; and in the Amazon, seeing bugs the size of small animals. But I was very trusting of people, sometimes *assuming* all would be okay.

We made it across the ice.

On our third day, after enjoying another lunch cooked by Bagii as we picnicked among the yellow grasses swaying in the breeze, we approached yet another of the numerous frozen rivers to be crossed. We could hear the ice breaking and feel the minibus slipping ever so slightly. My friend and I looked at each other as Mugii and Bagii started speaking in Mongolian.

Fear definitely took over!

Mugii revved the engine, putting the bus in several gears. I'm sure he was hoping to "jump" the vehicle to the other side. But what I knew about cars could be put on the top of a pin.

We were stuck and slipping in the middle of the river with about twenty feet on each side. Bagii assured us the river wasn't that deep, and that Mugii would get the minibus to the other side, and we would be safe.

What could we say?

He got out, surveying the damage, and we felt the bus slip a little more. Should we get out? But how? Was it safe? We knew the water was freezing.

They decided to get us out of the bus by piggybacking us to the other side. Mugii had tested the ice and said it was fine in the front where he would walk. He was a young guy, strapping, and easy on the eyes. He carried us effortlessly across the almost twenty feet to the dirt road.

This was not the first time I saw how strong Mongolian men were and, for that matter, the women as well. It was in their genes, Chinggis Khan, plus living in a harsh environment, you have to be tough. For six months the temperatures were well below zero F and the landscape was only white and brown. It was truly a land of survival of the fittest for both woman, man, and beast.

Mugii started to dig around the back wheel and attempted to prop it up with wood and rocks for traction. We all went in search of anything that could help him, making piles of different debris. I was amazed at how he was down in this icy water, getting soaked, and yet was not giving up. We heard a noise close by: a herd of goats and sheep wandered on the ice, foraging for any grasses they could find.

Typically, I had this Pollyanna attitude, but racing through my mind and my friend's as well was, *What are we going to do if he can't get the minibus out of the river?*

Now afternoon, and soon the temperature would start to drop even more, then what? Where would we spend the night? Or worse? Once you are out of UB, the rest of Mongolia is a scattering of small villages and gers.

Then like some magical story, a solitary horseman rode by on one of those small, but sturdy Mongolian horses. He didn't get down to help, but he spoke to Mugii for quite a while. Those were his sheep and goats foraging on the ice.

I'd been in Mongolia for only a couple of months and wasn't yet aware of the kinship Mongolians had for each other or how warm and very hospitable they were to foreign visitors. If it became necessary, a nomadic family would take us in, and we would spend the night in a ger with warmth and food. But then again, I didn't remember seeing any gers close by. But like in other remote areas of the world, sometimes things popped up out of thin air.

Magic?

By now, Mugii and Bagii were both soaked, trying to build up the back tires. When they thought they had the tires free, Mugii got into the minibus and tried to move it. I lost track of how many times this continued. He was also checking the engine, and I wasn't sure what else. Did I mention how little I knew about the running of cars?

Again Mugii got behind the wheel, while Bagii stood on the ice, letting him know what was going on. Finally the back tires came out of the water and onto the ice, like the spirit of Chinggis Khan was lifting them up. Mugii and the van charged for the other side and landed on the dirt road while we jumped up and down, hugging each other.

I was starting to believe in the power of the Khan. This was only the beginning of the transformative power that happened to me while in Mongolia—learning to believe in something beyond myself.

Unfazed as if this were a common occurrence, the goats and sheep still foraged on the ice.

We drove on to Dadal, twenty miles from the Russian border, a place that looked more like an alpine village, with log cabins instead of gers. It claimed to be the birthplace of Chinggis Khan. We stopped in the dark and had our picture taken next to a huge stone monument etched with his portrait commemorating his birthplace.

We gave thanks to the Khan for getting us out of the river. How bad could this guy be?

Two days later, after driving through the steppes covered in snow and ice, we got back to UB only to discover that the school was going to be closed for two more weeks because of a swine flu scare. It actually stayed closed a lot longer.

Was that a sign for another time, another flu? Another story.

CHAPTER 8

The Caretaker

Caretaker at Baldan Baraivan Monastery in Eastern Mongolia

His face was a road map. Not of superhighways or English country lanes, but of life. The sun and the extreme cold were etched into his brown skin as though Michelangelo had created and molded him.

He was a storyteller, and we were his audience. Everyone sat on the ground as he talked to my guide and driver. I didn't understand the Mongolian language, but he glanced my way, encouraging my participation with the excitement in his voice and gestures of his hands. He had told his story a thousand times, but it was a story worth telling. His life experience as a caretaker and guide at Baldan Baraivan Monastery in Eastern Mongolian. The monastery that had been destroyed by the Russians in the early 1900s and now was being rebuilt.

I knew he was leaving nothing out, the greatness and the sadness. Each of our stories always had the greatness and the sadness even if we didn't know.

I was traveling to Eastern Mongolia where the deep yellow grass went on forever, as did the blue sky: Chinggis Khan land. Some said that he was not only born there, but died there as well. The documentation was sketchy, his final resting place a mystery. Graverobbers and all that.

I was also a storyteller—maybe not like him, but I wanted to be. He was like my aunt and grandmother before me. His words flowed like a river not losing its course, and his voice transported me back in time when my aunt shared stories of when she and my uncle lived in one of those Caribbean islands in the 1940s—my uncle working for a US company. They said it was a dangerous place, because one never knew what the government might do. They had to be careful. But to my ears it was somehow exotic, mysterious.

Now I understood the mixture of fear and intrigue she must have felt, having had just returned myself to the US because of the worldwide pandemic, COVID-19. I had been teaching fourth grade at an international school in Phnom Penh, Cambodia, for six months when I felt it best to leave. I feared that if I waited too long, with all the restrictions, I might not be able to return to the US. A fate others had experienced.

Two worlds pulled me in different directions.

But it had always been that way for me. I didn't always

like it, but it was there, whether it was countries, people, or a sense of duty.

I never tired of listening to my aunt's stories, and now I knew it must have been difficult for them to return, and perhaps sharing her stories was cathartic.

It was soothing for me to share my recent experience about Cambodia, as if the words kept the memories alive. I didn't think my aunt realized, when she was sharing, that she was speaking to a young girl who had her own visions of adventure and travel, many times not sure of what to do, or where to go.

My grandmother's stories weren't of exotic places, but of everyday epiphanies. Hers was a life before her time. She never said that but, even as a child, I knew. Perhaps being a wife and a mother was not her first choice. I sometimes questioned that in myself. Frustrated that maybe I fulfilled someone else's wishes.

But I also learned it was never too late. Chances come in many forms if we keep our eyes open and our ears listening and let courage wrap itself around us like a soothing blanket.

I sensed their spirits—the same spirit inside me.

Was I like the caretaker, my aunt, and grandmother? Was I even in their category as my own grandkids listened to my stories of faraway travels and adventure—working to save cheetahs in Namibia, snorkeling the Great Barrier Reef, having a close encounter with a lion in Africa, teaching in Cambodia, riding a camel in Mongolia, to mention a few.

I watched the caretaker watch me. Was it because I was an American, and he was curious? Or did he know something about me that I didn't know?

CHAPTER 9

Gandan Monastery

Monks at Gandan Monastery in Ulaanbaatar, Mongolia

I watched as young and old, draped in their red robes, heads shaved, walk through old wooden doors dating back to the 1700s. They didn't seem to notice us mortals, but were focused on what was inside.

Fierce-looking creatures guarded the entrance. Did the monks' saintly ways preclude them from feeling what we mortals felt? For even when the weather was well below zero, I still saw them in the same robes, barely covered, walking the streets.

This Gandan Monastery in Ulaanbaatar had withstood

the Communist destruction of most Buddhist monasteries throughout Mongolia and the slaughter of thousands of Buddhists in the early 1900s. Now there were only a few monasteries throughout Mongolia, and only a small percentage of the population practiced Buddhism. It was different in Cambodia, which had hundreds of temples and pagodas, and 98 percent of the population practiced Buddhism. The monks wore orange robes as several sometimes crammed into a tuk-tuk, a motorized rickshaw, to get around the crowded city of Phnom Penh.

Before coming to Mongolia, I had never seen a Buddhist ceremony, so I was anxious to enter through those same doors, even with the scary-looking creatures. I watched and followed what others were doing. Taking my first steps, entering the inner sanctuary, felt holy, like those times growing up, when I sometimes felt close to God by stepping into my Catholic Church where I hoped answers would come, or at least peace would come to those problems that wouldn't leave me: arguments at home, boyfriends who weren't really boyfriends.

But here was no basin filled with Holy water, no crucifix with Christ, no candles to be lit; but the chanting and rhythmic beating of the drums, a meditative quality that felt holy, otherworldly. Soothing. Peaceful.

I watched what others did and, when the time was right, I circled clockwise around the temple inside, pausing at the front to place money at the feet of Buddha, asking for guidance, hoping my prayers would be heard and answered, like I did so many years before in that Catholic Church. I knew others were also seeking answers, guidance—I saw it on their faces, even if there were no tears. Anguish and sadness are universal.

I made my way from the front of the temple to the back. When I exited, I walked backward to get some distance between me and the Buddha before turning my back. Once

31

outside I found the prayer wheels I spun to offer more blessings and to seek answers.

I didn't consider myself a religious person, but definitely spiritual. I had questions and sometimes doubts, but I always found comfort and solace when I visited the Buddhist monasteries in Mongolia. A few years back when I was touring through Tuscany with my good friends, we stopped at the churches, small and large. My Catholic upbringing didn't leave me as I lit candles, sending love to my son, hoping our relationship would heal. But I had also learned the Universe's time and my time were not the same.

CHAPTER 10

White Cliffs

White Cliffs in the Gobi Desert

Were these creations by kings and queens from galaxies beyond our imagination?

Gothic cathedrals, fortresses, hidden chambers carved deep in iridescent stone, holding secrets and treasures they knew no one would ever find, as though the end product had been sprinkled with red and gold fairy dust, or perhaps painted with fine brush strokes by the master of old.

How could this place be of this planet? Had climate change bypassed this extraordinary place, leaving it untouched by the world's turmoil?

Another world?

Maybe it opened up to both hell and heaven. I was afraid to stand on the precipice, because the wind was blowing fiercely; but we watched our guide walk out and stand on the edge. I was afraid of being swept off; I was afraid for her. I didn't want her to know how fearful I was; I didn't want anyone to know. But like so many things in our lives, the sheer drop also held a certain fascination.

I had acrophobia, the fear of heights, the fear of jumping off a cliff, a high place. Though a common phobia, knowing that didn't make me feel any better. I discovered the malady years ago on a trip with my sister through France. We stopped at one of those Roman aqueducts. I followed my sister through a maze of stairs to the top and, as we both emerged to walk along this stone platform which was about ten feet wide with no railings on either side, I panicked and had to immediately sit down, scoot myself back to the stairs, and get on solid ground.

My sister, who seemed to have no fear of anything, kept walking. How two sisters from the same family could be so different, I didn't know.

My fear was not simply the height with no protection, but also the feeling I might jump. Occasionally, it still happened to me, and I wondered how a sane person could have these feelings.

But the beauty of the place made me fantasize that, if I did let go, perhaps I would sprout wings and become birdlike, a creature that could fly inside the darkness as well as the light, discovering secrets that alluded humans.

I was brave, but not that brave!

This was the Gobi Desert of southern Mongolia, the White Cliffs, where you can find volcanic red rock, dinosaur fossils as well as shells from an ancient ocean, stones that seemingly came from a rainbow. Roy Chapman Andrews, an American explorer who led expeditions into the Gobi Desert in the early twentieth century, made important discoveries of fossil dinosaur eggs. Some said the Indiana Jones character was patterned after him.

If you are really lucky, you might spot the elusive snow leopard, a solitary animal that maybe was a guardian of those who created this magical place. But I never saw one.

And so the Gobi Desert remained a mystery like other things in Mongolia. But wasn't mystery and magic what we all sought? What made us stronger and who we really were?

I was hoping.

CHAPTER 11

Jeremiah Johnson

When we arrived in October in the Eastern Gobi, it was the beginning of the off-season at Ikh Nart National Park, home to mountain goats and bighorn sheep. It was only me, my driver and guide, and the ranger who was a sort of Mongolian Jeremiah Johnson—a mysterious loner. At least to me. A little rougher around the edges than Gobi motorcycle guy, but still.

I watched him.

I didn't want anyone to know I was watching. But my eyes were following his movements as though I had no choice.

They spoke Mongolian—Jeremiah Johnson, my guide and driver. When necessary, my guide interpreted for me.

I sensed an ease between them, like old friends who occasionally saw each other; the familiarity was there. Throughout my years in Mongolia, I felt this ease between the people as though they all knew each other, and in some cases they did. With it being the size of Alaska, only three million people and landlocked, Mongolians did know ease. A foreign concept to many of us Americans.

During the tourist season, Jeremiah Johnson was busy; but now with the end of the season, he was alone for the most part. Occasionally a herder stopped by for a night or two. On this particular night, it was a woman herder with her goats. After a dinner of rice, meat, and a small salad, I left them and went back to my ger, listening to their laughter, a little envious.

We stayed two breathtaking nights in this beautiful remote place. I spent a lot of time exploring and hiking the rugged terrain. With no other visitors, it reminded me of my times exploring in Africa, except here there were no real predators—no lions, no venomous snakes, no annoying and scary baboons.

Occasionally, late at night, I heard a wolf off in the distance; and during the day, vultures came if there was carrion. I watched bighorn sheep scale the mountains with no effort at all.

Once on safari in Tanzania, I decided to hike up this hill, the camp manager telling me that I would be okay because predators slept during the day. Did I really listen to him? After getting to the top, fear took over, and I raced down, only to glance back as baboons suddenly appeared where I had been standing. I kept going.

I had always been in awe of nature. Especially as I looked at the Indian-red rock formations surrounding our camp, they looked as if someone had sculptured the scene and placed them in exactly the right way—it couldn't be by chance, could it? A Mongolian Stonehenge was created by high priests or rather monks clothed in red robes. At night I was sure a famous artist had painted a full, orange moon so big in the night sky, I thought I could reach out and touch it and maybe learn what it was made of. I pictured those same monks worshipping the moon late into the night. I was tempted to leave my ger in search of those monks and the secrets that I knew were hidden in those stones.

On my last trip to Africa, to Namibia, to work with cheetahs at a conservation refuge, I remembered walking outside at two a.m. to use the bathroom, and when I opened the door to our little hut, I stopped dead in my tracks because the sky was so lit up with thousands and thousands of stars; it took my breath away. Like a dazzling, white blanket someone had thrown over, mesmerizing.

In that moment, I didn't care about snakes, lions, or what else was out there in the night.

Was Jeremiah Johnson glad he didn't live in the city? Did he know what a treasure he had? I did, and I thought he did also.

Bad boys always knew more than they let on.

CHAPTER 12

Gers

Gers in the Gobi Desert

I sometimes lost myself in the vastness of this place. That it seemed to go on forever was what I liked and, even more, it was what my spirit needed. I wanted to believe that it never ended, like space, like the ocean, like the mountains where I wondered what was on the other side of the peak. I thought it was the unknown that captured me, not knowing, not wanting to know.

I took long walks, venturing further and further, possibly to see what was beyond the beyond. I was not afraid; in fact,

I was more at home in these secret places, whether they were real or existed in my imagination. The family rides through the woods of New Jersey always came back to me, where I invented the mythical creatures that one could barely see unless you went deeper and deeper in the woods. Unless you were me.

Not long ago, I spent a few months in Dolzago, Italy, not too far from Milan, teaching English to a family. When they were at work, I went into the small town and then up in the hills, soon discovering what I labeled a secret garden. I fantasized that it was like the book, *The Secret Garden*. However, this garden had a locked gate that I didn't open. But that made it all-the-more enchanting. As I walked to the top of the hill, I soon found an abandoned castle attached to the garden. This became my adventure, my fantasy almost daily.

After enjoying a cappuccino and a little sweet pastry at my favorite patisserie in town, I walked to the top and found a spot to eat my brioche and think about what occurred at the castle and the garden more than a hundred years ago.

One day I discovered an old church near the castle and a young couple dancing. We exchanged pleasantries, but I never saw them again after that day.

I always used a walking stick and, when I finally left Dolzago, I left the stick propped up against a stone near the locked gate of the secret garden, perhaps for another traveler, or thinking I might return years later and find the stick still there.

The Gobi Desert of Mongolia: not a place to fear, but to embrace. To be where the only road wasn't a freeway, but a dirt one, was exhilarating. A much-needed respite from homes butted up to one another, bumper to bumper traffic that snaked on forever, noise.

We stayed in a ger, a simple Mongolian home, with one room and no window, a small door facing south, which allowed for light, the warmth of the southern sun, and protection from the wind. Camels right outside always held their heads high in a regal fashion. The stove inside was for cooking and additional heat.

The ger had an influential role in shaping the Mongolian character and family life. The small confines prevent privacy, but compel families to interact, sharing everything, making families stronger.

When entering a ger, we always moved in a clockwise direction. When seated, the hosts served us milk tea with salt, biscuits or *aaruul*, Mongolian curd cheese, which was one of the main foods of the Mongolian nomadic people, and very high in protein, helping to fortify the body against the cold winter.

More recently I spent time at Angor Wat, the mysterious temples in northern Cambodia. Because of COVID, I was there without tourists. At times, embracing the solitude, I almost felt transported back to when they were created.

Could I be a type of Indiana Jones or Jeremiah Johnson? I do like my creature comforts. But could I return to these places for short periods of time and be that girl who sought the mysteries of the woods, the secret garden, the never-ending desert, the temples?

I sometimes forgot, but then I told myself, *There was a time, a time I was actually in the Gobi, at the garden gate, in the temples of Angkor Wat, up close and personal with the lions at the Ngorongoro Crater.*

There was a time . . .

CHAPTER 13

Hauling Water

I thought kids were the same all over the world. At least, that'd been my experience teaching in the US, Mongolia, East Timor, and Cambodia.

They were friendly, always waving. In many cases, "Hi!' was the only English word they knew. Even the little ones yelled it out, their big smiles from ear to ear as if an artist penciled them in. I, of course, said, "Hi!" back, giving them my biggest smile.

Wherever I walked—around school, downtown—the Mongolian kids stared at me. I knew there was a fascination for both of us about our differences. Maybe they didn't completely understand the pull. Sometimes I didn't either, but my blue eyes seemed to be what they all stared at, that and my white hair in the later years.

"Grandmas don't leave their country and teach in another country," some said in a respectful way. *Weren't we supposed to stay home, be close by, and watch the grandkids?* I knew that was what some were thinking.

Echoes of words from some of my family and friends. Not always understanding I was gypsy woman, gypsy mom, and the wanderlust was a calling I cannot ignore. That I was an eternal beginner does not bother me. Apparently it never had except in the recesses of my mind where the fight always took place. But another beginning, yet another start. And why not!

Some say, "Mothers are supposed to settle down, mellow, accept their lives."

It is painful at times to be true to yourself. I constantly fought the old tapes from childhood, especially from my mother about what a woman should be, and not be. She grew up in a different generation where our identity was sometimes lost as we said, "I do!"

I wonder at this point in my life, in my seventies, *Will I fight this fight for the rest of my life?* I thought of all the women before me, the trailblazers, had they said the same thing? Of course they had! We were not done with this by any means, but that didn't stop us.

These children, some as young as five who carted water containers, lived with their families in gers close to my international school and close to very expensive apartment buildings. Gers were round circular homes made of felt and canvas, originating with the nomadic lifestyle of the Mongolians out in the countryside. However, now we found these homes in the overpopulated capital city of UB. People looked for jobs because the nomadic herders were giving way to the urban nomads, thinking there was more money to be made in UB than in herding sheep or goats.

Because there was no running water in the gers, the children hauled rolling containers to a water station every day so they could buy water, fill them up, and haul them back to their gers. The gers weren't hooked up to the sewage system for the city, so they used outhouses or whatever was convenient.

The contrasts between the lifestyles in Mongolia and Southern California were something new to me. I grew up in middle America where the basic necessities and beyond were met. Yes, I traveled to many developing countries, but this was my first time living in one. I didn't want to judge what was all around me, but I knew I did, especially when I saw children pushing carts that weighed more than them, selling food on the streets.

I thought about the words, "white privilege." I didn't like being in that category, but I knew I was.

But still living five years in Mongolia, and then East Timor and Cambodia, changed me, changed my perspective on life and what was important.

Again, as one Mongolian said to me, "You like it here. I think you've become Mongolian."

What did the children think of us, of me? Could our smiles and the friendly hellos between us get us past our differences so that being human was all that really mattered?

I wanted this to be true. I'd seen it happen . . . and happen in my own life.

We called them street kids because they had street smarts. You could see it in their eyes. We laughed, because we knew they could survive much better than we could! I admired them, not in the "white privilege" way, but because they were genuine. Something I strived for in myself.

I thought of my own grandkids who were around ten and thirteen years old then, and how, quite frankly, I would never refer to them as "street kids."

CHAPTER 14

Graffiti

Graffiti in Ulaanbaatar

The reflection in the window made it seem that much more daunting. The eyes almost vacant and perhaps looking beyond to something I could not see or feel. A life I had never experienced, and yet intriguing.

On this particular fall day, with the weather still nice and the sun shining, I was with a group of photographers, some like me: amateurs, but a few professionals and a mixture of expats and Mongolians. Our goal was to capture the heartbeat of the capital city of UB.

We were drawn, of course, to the typical cityscapes, land-scapes, and people. But something else caught our eyes.

I wasn't aware until I had done some research that graffiti has existed since ancient times, dating back to ancient Egypt, ancient Greece, and the Roman Empire.

The graffiti scene in UB emerged in the late 1990s after the fall of communism. Freedom brought many things—a place to express yourself wherever or whatever that might be.

She was Mongolian, wearing traditional clothes and headdress from centuries ago. Royalty? Again the eyes drew me in with their carefully penciled outline, not unlike the Egyptians. What was she thinking? Or better yet, what was the artist thinking?

Women in ancient Mongolia were not just ornaments and housekeepers. They were held in high regard in their society, especially in the early ages; and they enjoyed a great deal of freedom compared to women in other cultures at the time. An example was that Mongol women had the right to refuse marriage. This was extremely rare in ancient times. Another example was the wives of Chinggis Khan had their own personal courts called Ordo.

Chinggis Khan's mother, Hoelun, kept her children alive on wild root vegetables and what game they could find, despite being left for dead by her tribe after her husband was murdered by a rival clan.

Mongol women were expected to be physically strong and organized as the nomadic lifestyle required quick setup and take down of the gers, control of the herds of animals such as horses and sheep, as well as cooking and raising children.

I once saw a Mongolian woman in her thirties pick up a small refrigerator and move it all by herself!

Are eyes really the windows to the soul? Cicero was quoted saying, "The face is a picture of the mind as the eyes are its interpreter."

If I were on the inside of the window, looking out, would her presence on the wall be the same or simply another piece of graffiti? Would I see her as an independent woman as I wanted her to be as well as myself? Women past and present who I knew fought the same fight.

Alexandra David-Neel was a Belgian-French explorer and in 1924, when she was fifty-six years old, she visited Tibet when it was forbidden to foreigners, and especially women. I yearned to be like this woman, like the Mongolian women—independent, without fear.

I glanced back at her face—was that a sly wink I saw?

CHAPTER 15

The Road Less Traveled

Truly the road less traveled. This was how I always pictured myself—with nothing before me except the open road. Only tire tracks. It could be the open ocean or a mountain that went on forever, or even outer space. Had I been transported to Mars? That was what this empty desert looked like. What was beyond the stars? I was sure other life, maybe similar to us, but not us. What about the concept of time? If only I could speak with H. G. Wells. I was saddened by the fact I would not live long enough to know these things.

But maybe.

I was like my father; we were nomads. It was hard to keep us from not wandering; I was sure that was how my mother felt about my dad. During WWII, he was in the Navy and traveled the seas on a minesweeper, a small warship designed to remove or detonate naval mines to keep waterways clear for safe shipping.

Whoa! I thought.

I never got tired of hearing him tell his story. "I saw a large object coming toward the ship and I thought *Oh! My God, it's a torpedo, and I'm going to die.* But then as it got closer, I saw that it was only a porpoise that disappeared under when it reached the ship."

At home he would put us in the car and explore whether it was the woods in New Jersey or the snow-covered mountains in Southern California. Visions of my mother hanging onto the door handle as though that would keep us from sliding down the mountain. One time he was driving by himself and got so distracted that he drove into a ditch.

I am a road warrior exactly like him.

I wished we had talked about how similar we were. He would love that I traveled the world and was not afraid to try new things.

But we never had that talk. Instead, at times it seemed we were more at odds with each other than anything else.

And then he died way too young.

I like to think that who he was lived on in who I am. When others ask about my travels and experiences, I always mention that I am very much like my dad.

When I returned to Mongolia in 2014, I had started my blog and named it, *The Wandering Nomad.*

It was going to be my last year teaching at my international school, and I was leaving Mongolia, so I wanted to make this special: me and the Gobi Desert. I traveled with only a guide and a driver.

I had my own ger, and on this particular night, my guide asked if I wanted more coal in the stove to keep me warm while I was sleeping.

I said, "Of course!"

Mistake, big mistake. It became so hot inside the ger that I couldn't sleep, I felt like I was suffocating. So I stripped down to my bra and undies and tried to get some of the coal out of the stove, which was another big mistake, and very dangerous. I resorted to opening the small ger door and sitting at the door even though a party was going on in the next ger, and people were wandering about. I didn't care if they saw me; I was more concerned with breathing and living.

Well after midnight, the coal started to lose its heat, and the cool air enveloped the inside.

Ah! Finally sleep, my beating heart echoed.

Once again, I was carried away with the mystery and intrigue of this never-ending desert. The mystery I was beginning to see was keeping me safe.

CHAPTER 16

The Boy Goat Herder

Few tourists traveled to the eastern part of the Gobi near Ikh Nart National Park. Because some did, he was familiar with our ways, cameras and phones clicking away. Familiar with our differences even if he wasn't sure what they all meant. His dark eyes, taking it all in.

He was four years old and had already learned from his parents how to herd sheep and goats, a craft he would pass on to his children. No question.

We were all up early, too early to eat because there were jobs to be done. I brushed my teeth in the makeshift bowl with no running water, and found water to splash on my face as I applied some lotion. If people back home could only see me.

Roaming between the goats like the city dweller I am, I watched him as he watched me. His curiosity refreshing. I came from a world that many times didn't have patience with the everyday. Life here was all about patience.

The mother motioned me over as she milked a goat, "Did I want to try?" As she pulled on the teats, she didn't ask me in English or even Mongolian, but some things didn't require words.

I tried, but not with much success. I thought I heard a few chuckles. I was wondering what the goat was thinking. I always thought it important when I traveled to at least try. In Namibia, while working at a cheetah refuge center, I fed the cheetahs while cleaning up their poop; and in Botswana,

51

I went on a walking safari with a guide who carried a big stick and told us, "If I tell you to climb up a tree, or run, do it; there's a reason."

The best part was when the mother was done, she hugged me and asked the guide to take our photo.

Sometimes he was part little boy with snot smudged across his face, waiting for me to take a photo as he played with his cat; and other times he was part man as he imitated his father's hands clasped behind his back, walking the perimeter of the yard, making sure all was well. He showed me how important his task was by climbing rocks to scan the horizon. Goat herding like sheepherding involved a lot of walking and sitting, watching the goats and the sky, making sure they didn't stray too far. Important lessons for the family's survival as one day he would be the father and in charge.

At times like these, I wished I knew more of the Mongolian language so I could talk to him. But Mongolia was teaching me different ways to communicate. Sometimes the eyes said it all.

Once again, I was reminded of the street kids back in UB that I knew could survive better than I could. My own grandkids have a different kind of "smarts," not better, just different.

I looked into those dark eyes, wondering what he thought of us—these travelers from faraway, from a place he'll probably never see. But then again all things were possible, aren't they?

The Mongolian children were always my favorite. I didn't always understand why, but it was true.

CHAPTER 17

Mongolian Contortionists

Mongolian Contortionists

They moved slowly as one, somehow connected physically and spiritually mesmerizing their audience when no sound could be heard, swaying with a primal beat that drew in the audience. Bodies twisted into strange and unnatural shapes and positions. Strong muscles. Beautiful iridescent costumes, perfect makeup, and hair.

Did they know where one began and the other ended? I lost myself in not only watching them, but remembering . . .

A young child dancing in her bedroom, spinning round, trying to imitate the movements of the dancers I watched on TV, and practicing pirouettes. Ballet lessons and then the ultimate as a teenager—semi-private, private lessons with a hard-core Russian instructor who carried a stick. She was unafraid to demand what she wanted. Her desire scared and fascinated me. I wanted to want that way. I wanted to please her, and myself. So I endured whatever it took.

Promises of being on toe, wanting it, and then the first time: the agony, the pain, the sweat pouring down between my small breasts. Every inch of my body was wet.

But the freedom was as addicting as any drug. I didn't want to stop.

I wanted to dance.

In high school, along with a close friend, we introduced modern dance and performed for the entire school, each losing ourselves in the movement, in the music, in the moment.

There was nothing like it.

I wanted to go to Broadway as a dancer. Teachers encouraged me. "We'll see your name in lights," they said. But the competition was fierce, so I let the dream go.

In my twenties, after having my children, I tried to take up dancing, but it wasn't the same—or was it; I wasn't the same—or was I?

So I watched these performers with a longing.

Did they have the same feelings I once had, that I still had?

My camera was clicking away, but I was a shadow on stage with them dancing and moving the way they were moving—the way I moved when I was young and the dancer. Could they sense me? Of course, they did. Maybe our eyes did not connect, but the soul was alive as ever, leaving footprints on my heart so that once again I was changed forever.

The years had moved on, the muscles stiff, but the dance was still in me. I sometimes dreamed and sometimes danced in my living room to an imaginary audience, to a song in my heart. Years seemed to fall away as my arms and hands flowed gracefully, practicing my plies, spins, and maybe an arabesque, making sure I didn't bump into furniture.

Mongolian contortionism dated back to the thirteenth century to the time of Chinggis Khan and was performed primarily by girls or young women. Now girls as young as nine could spend four hours a day in training, learning to bend and doubling over—seemingly defying nature. Mongolian contortionists were in high demand internationally.

We were invited by the owner of the international school where I was teaching to this performance at a Torgol Show downtown UB.

Did I know I would have to travel 6,000 miles to, once again, be the dancer?

CHAPTER 18

First Day of School

They came looking like they were going to a ball—girls and boys from kindergarten to high school. The younger students dressed in their red-and-black uniforms. The first day of school was for me the first day of teaching at an international school. I looked around, wondering about my new first graders, about teaching foreign students in a foreign country for the first time. But as I strolled through the sea of students, parents, and grandparents with huge smiles, holding dozens of bouquets of flowers the colors of the rainbow, I was quickly moved to tears. Was this a wedding? But then again, it was so much more: like a new dawn breaking for students and those who loved them.

And for me—a new beginning. I would learn one of many.

Not having a new beginning was what always scared me, not the beginning.

His face was beautiful; there was no other way to say it. Smooth like porcelain rubbed to perfection, high cheekbones. He could have been Michael Jackson, the way he wore the glitzy fedora like one who had worn a fedora many times before. He could have been a model. But he was neither; he was a student getting ready to meet his new teacher.

His almost-black eyes were looking at something in the distance, or maybe not. The eyes were what held me, even though he never looked at me or the camera. Even at his young age, he had a presence—a presence that I would discover over the years was part of being Mongolian. Young and old had a noble sense of pride. I was reminded of Native Americans.

"Was it born from Chinggis Khan?" I asked myself that first day.

Now I knew it was. But at the time, I didn't know that much about the Khan except all the negative information I read in my history books. I was new and didn't understand. Not a good excuse.

But then I found many positive things written about Chinggis Khan—one of history's greatest military leaders uniting tribes, changing the roles of women.

The Khan was in their blood, and one felt it.

This young man's face was always in my mind's eye, reflecting on the faces of the children I taught, the street kids who said hello in English as I walked by, and the kids in the countryside whose faces were sometimes darker, but the eyes were still the same.

He vanished from my sight as I took my place at the front of the school as my own first graders brought me flowers, holding them like a precious commodity, as if I was precious.

I never knew his name nor his grade, and I don't remember seeing him again, but I will always remember his eyes, his poise, and the fedora.

CHAPTER 19

Buddhist Statue

Buddhist Statue in Zaisan

He was smiling, I thought. Perfectly carved with flowing, gold robes. Did the religious statues back home in America smile? I didn't think so. Instead they were always looking serious, even scary, tired, hopeless, somber. I've been in enough churches in my life to know this for a fact.

I hardly knew anything about Buddhism when I first arrived in Mongolia for my two-year teaching contract. But I was drawn to this statue that stood tall and not dwarfed by other buildings, but simply a sprinkling of businesses and gers, the nomadic homes of the Mongolians. However, over the years, change occurred in this area of Zaisan, the "suburb" of UB where my school was located.

The statue was a beacon, a lighthouse, not for ships sailing in the night, but for people. Possibly a Buddhist Statue of Liberty that you could see for miles—*Give me your tired, your poor, your huddled masses . . .*

But who were they?

My friends and I came to the foot of the statue and circled three times, asking for blessings as though we were lighting candles or dipping fingers in Holy water and making the sign of the cross. Maybe one of us was carrying a rosary or worry beads.

I was raised Catholic, so I knew the drill. Old habits don't die.

But he wasn't a scary-looking Jesus on a cross with blood dripping.

At the end I uttered, *Namaste*, being told he healed everything, especially broken hearts and bad karma, relationships that weren't what they seemed. The darkest moments.

The red/orange-robed monks came, their arms bare even in the middle of winter when it could be minus 20F. Did they spin the prayer wheels, asking for their own blessing?

I thought so; I did. I was always looking for answers, storing them up like some squirrel. One never knew.

When I returned to UB after three years, I was pleasantly surprised that he was still there in his same spot, almost defying the tall buildings that threaten to hide his smile and dwarf his presence. But not so.

What did he think of progress?

And still they came.

If you listen and don't whisper a word, you might hear him chanting, bringing a peace that only chanting could bring. Taking away the fear, replacing it with hope and peace.

Bogd Khan Mountain was a sacred place and the backdrop for this Buddhist statue. A protected forest that I was sure held many secrets, as I was sure his smile did as well. From school it was a short hike up into this sacred area, a place I visited as often as possible being the squirrel that I was.

I felt the pull as I got closer.

I still went inside a church, especially when I traveled, dipping my fingers in holy water, making the sign of the cross, lighting candles, believing it helped because it had.

I felt solace looking up into his smile, feeling the goodness as I circled three times.

It didn't matter where or what country, I saw the monks or the color of their robes, and when I saw them, I felt that soothing peace. My breath slowed down.

Once again I said, "Namaste," realizing my broken heart was no more.

CHAPTER 20

The First Snow

The land was void of all life as if aliens had swept down and removed what had been there. What color you could see was not of nature—no green grass or blooming pink flowers. But it was still beautiful in a surreal way and a tad bit frightening as we stared out through our school window secure in our room that sheltered us from the bitter cold and the white that covered the playground. However, I knew the first graders wanted to feel the snow on their faces, to run and play.

I was new to this, with fleeting memories as a seven-year-old living in New Jersey. I watched from my living room window as the sky turned black. My mother said, "A big storm is coming." Was she scared?

I didn't think I was, even when the white blizzard hit. I had been more intrigued with the black sky. So maybe I wanted to touch the white as much as these little first graders.

Kids are the same everywhere.

For a long time, we just watched, faces glued to the windows as the scene gradually unfolded, snow covering every inch of land to the barely visible Zaisan Memorial up on the mountain, to the roofs of the gers across the street, as though a magician had waved a magic wand or spoken an incantation.

The kids got antsy.

We couldn't put on our Mongolian winter coats fast enough, scarves flew as we ran outside, barely getting gloves and hats on as we turned our faces toward an unseen power as the softness kissed us, and we hardly noticed the cold melting against our skin. We watched as our breath became alive.

I was sure I was seven again with not a care in the world.

Already students were making a snowman. Excitement sparked around their faces with only their dark-brown eyes showing.

The snow came fast with a vengeance as many things did in Mongolia and stayed for six months. At the time, I didn't know it would lose its pristine whiteness and become dirty, black until it all melted. Stained yellow with urine. When you were young, it didn't seem to matter. But being older and "stuck" inside my small apartment tried my patience to the point I considered leaving and never returning. A nomad searching for warmth and color.

But at that moment, I was caught up again as a youngster when something is new and exciting. Fear hadn't got its grip on me, not at seven.

Over the five years I lived in Mongolia, I made my peace with the white. Perhaps that was all it asked, and that I remember the excitement and not lose sight of what was really important. To be that child again, even if I couldn't physically, the yearning in my heart was still there. And wasn't that what we are all seeking?

On that day after returning to class, excitement was in the air, innocence with all. So we made snowflakes from white and colored paper. The children's laughter filled the room with promises. And filled me with memories and hope.

CHAPTER 21

Outhouses

Outhouse in Mongolia

I took photos of churches and museums, but I liked the unusual: outhouses and old doors. Having used many outhouses
throughout Mongolia as well as Africa, South America, other

parts of Asia, and some parts of Europe, I certainly appreciate what I have at home.

However, with that said, I always follow the motto, "When in Rome, do as the Romans do." Consequently, my butt has been on more seats than what I can remember, or maybe want to remember.

I laughed, "Is there a standard blueprint with merely materials changing?"

Some used all wood, others all tin, and some a combination. And different colors—red, blue, were very common. Most were singular, but I had seen two together. They were built far away from the family's gers for obvious reasons, but within walking distance. The doors never really closed and, once inside, you had to have the skills of an acrobat to balance what needed to be done without falling through the slates and going down. "Oh! God!" I remember shouting. I didn't go down, but just *looking* down brought fear and anxiety.

The smell thing was not a problem for me because, throughout my entire life as far back as I could remember, I'd never had a sense of smell. People asked me to smell a flower, and I nodded and said, "Yeah, that's nice," not really smelling anything. I thought that was what everyone experienced. It came in handy when changing diapers, but not so handy when my husband at the time walked into our home and yelled, "Get out of the house! Can't you smell the gas? It's everywhere!" Consequently, I checked burners all the time.

I used the outhouses during the day, but at night the nearest piece of dirt outside the ger felt the safest. Many times, the best show was late at night. If I was lucky, I might see a yellow-orange moon so big I thought, or maybe hoped, I could take it for a ride. Another time, a sky had stars that outnumbered what I thought the sky could hold. Red rock stones looking like Stonehenge, pillars standing guard.

Years ago I traveled to Istanbul, and the only toilet in the restaurant was that delightful Turkish toilet on the ground with foot rests, but no seat. That would have been okay, but it was located right in the eating area, behind a door that had a two-way mirror where I could see all the men eating within very close proximity. I knew they couldn't see me, but still!

Oh! The places you could pee!

CHAPTER 22

Khamar Monastery

Energy Center in the Eastern Gobi Desert

I had just walked into the Khamar Monastery in the Gobi when I saw a little boy dressed in the traditional Buddhist clothing, even wearing the Mongolian boots with the turned-up toe to protect the earth. *What was behind those liquid black eyes and the almost devious smile?* I wondered. Eyes are the window to the soul—so it is said. *Is he looking into my soul? Is he already blessed by the gods? Is he wondering if I was?*

He took his time fixing his hat, so I waited with my camera. As always, I asked permission. He was used to the tourists from foreign lands and, as he adjusted his hat, he glanced a peek at me to see if I was still paying attention. His smile was infectious.

About half the monks were young boys who studied Tibetan Buddhism. The practice of Buddhism was the never-ending humbling of the ego. I was told it was an honor for a young boy to be chosen. It seemed similar to a priesthood in the Catholic church. When my cousin became a priest, he said he knew from the time he was very young that that was what he wanted to be.

I only knew I wanted to be a movie star/dancer.

Maybe knowing was all that mattered, or maybe not. Maybe finding was more important.

We had come from Black Mountain and the Energy Center, both places close by and very sacred to the Mongolians and the Buddhists. Places they believe you could receive good and positive energy from the earth and spiritual serenity. Buddhists believe in a legendary kingdom called Shambala in Central Asia—a quiet place where all the inhabitants could live in joy and harmony. Mongolians think the entry to Shambala was near Khamar Monastery. Many people from all over the world make pilgrimages there to receive this spiritual serenity.

I was always looking for joy and harmony in my life, especially at that moment, because I was leaving Mongolia in a few months to return to Southern California, and not sure what I wanted to do, where I wanted to be. I decided to give it a go, so outside I laid down on the red sandstone, hoping the fiery soil would bring me warmth and answers.

As I was trying to relax, I looked over and not too far away was my driver, also lying down. It was quiet, peaceful, with hardly anyone around. Instead of fighting the moment, I found myself drifting off in a sort of meditative state. Whether I fell asleep or not, I wasn't sure; but I knew I didn't

67

want to get up. The peace I sometimes sought had enveloped me with a kind of warmth that I didn't want to leave. Answers to my future were still out there. But maybe the peace was all I needed for the moment.

As we were leaving the monastery, I saw one of my favorite student's grandparents who had traveled all the way from UB. They were excited to see me as I was to see them; we shared stories about their granddaughter.

Blessings and answers came in many forms.

CHAPTER 23

Adventure

I guess there is more than one way to get clean.

Walking back to school after having a delicious mocha at one of my favorite coffee places, Tom N Toms, I spotted this little boy around four years old. Log cabins were very unusual in this part of Mongolia, more prevalent in the north with its forests. But of course, what really caught my eye was the kid, and the bathtub outside.

Could you wash more things besides the kid, maybe goats, maybe clothes? Maybe all together? And why not?

He seemed oblivious to anything beyond the tub. He kept looking down, but not at me. I wasn't that close; I didn't want to intrude. Was there water? Maybe he was hoping for water, waiting for an adult to finish the job.

I thought that, like any kid anywhere, he found fascination in what adults might think was mundane. One of the reasons I liked to teach children was because of their innocence. We lose that as we get older. The ability to live and be in the moment. To laugh. To live in Kairos and not Chronos. I wanted to believe I had a balance between the two, but the truth was: I was many times rushing time as though I knew best.

He was perched on the window sill, legs dangling, then almost wrapped around the clothesline, fiddling with a clothespin. "*Aha*," I said to myself. *Also used for clothes.*

I didn't want to stare too long, but the tub didn't look

secure, at least to my eyes. It made me think about my mother and my aunt. Sisters, but entirely different. My aunt would have fit right in with Mongolian life; my mother would have run the other way.

My parents moved to California from New Jersey when I was eight, and my brother was five. They and my baby sister left later in the summer, while my brother and I left right after school was done and traveled with my aunt and uncle by car all across the US.

I mark it as my first real adventure.

We were in the car; it was summer and it was hot. No air conditioning. It was 1953. Not sure what state we were in, but I had on the least amount of clothes, because of the heat and humidity. Periodically my aunt gave us salt tablets to help with dehydration. I liked this adventure. I was drinking an orange juice, and my uncle went over a bump that caused my sticky, sugary juice to spill in my hair and other parts. I looked down and orange was everywhere. I thought my aunt would freak out because that was what my mother would do; but she didn't. Much to my surprise and happiness, she passed me a rag and said, "You'll be fine. We'll clean up later."

Right then I knew I liked this lady.

I walked on, leaving that little boy to whatever adventure he was in.

CHAPTER 24

Starting Over Again

When I was at a party and people found out what I'd done, I usually had to repeat because they did that double-take thing almost like Linda Blair in *The Exorcist*.

They usually said, "You've done what and where?"

If they were really brave, they asked, "Why?"

The why was always the hardest. It was easy to spout off what I did and then give them a geography lesson on the location of Mongolia. I saw it on their faces—the embarrassment of not knowing where Mongolia was located. But, hey, we all knew the poor scores of American students on geography compared to other countries.

The hardest was explaining why. How much to tell? Life-changing circumstances. How detailed to get? Divorcing, yet again. How much did people really want to know? Sort of like writing a memoir. I didn't want to cry in my beer, but . . .

Divorcing after retiring and not sure about income. Of course, all my friends, and even those acquaintances who maybe didn't want all the details, they all knew. I was like a lot of women who felt the need to share. Didn't it bond us as a group? Oprah stuff. But I knew I didn't want to be married anymore, I didn't want to wait as long as I did the first time, when I was turned inside out, and one day looked in the mirror and asked, "Who are you?"

Was it worse the second time, because one thought one had learned?

But the fact was, I found myself in my sixties, separated, with a divorce in the near future, retired, and did I say I retired counting on the income from my soon-to-be ex? That all happened around the holidays, which sent me into that dark area of depression. I remember meeting my son and his family at a local outdoor mall to enjoy the huge Christmas tree, and I got out of my car and a panic attack seized me so violently that I had to get back into the car. I wondered if I should call 911. Let me just say up front that divorcing him was a good thing, but still! I needed a job. What to do? I was almost embarrassed to admit any of this because, after all, this was my second time in this arena. I didn't know why I felt the need to always be counting anything and everything. It was as though I was in a game, and either who had the most or the least wins. A very dear friend once told me, "I have friends who are on their third and fourth marriages. So what!"

So I put on my big-girl panties and, after the first of the year, I met with a close friend who helped me with my resume. I was shocked to see that I really had accomplished quite a lot; maybe someone would hire me. During our initial meeting, he asked me what I had always wanted to do. Sheepishly I said, "Live and work in another country."

I was not sure what his next words were, but something to the effect that that was what I needed to do. But even without his words, I knew it in my heart as soon as I said it. So I embarked on an almost four-month odyssey, trying to find work in another country. I was a novice at this, but I was a good researcher and was not afraid to ask people for help and/or guidance: a female Homer. I didn't realize it at the time, but courage was already wrapping itself around me like a warm blanket, changing me forever.

I was a teacher, and I found two organizations that acted

as recruiters for teachers to teach in other countries. *Voila!!!* But before that I just sent my resume out to what seemed like hundreds of schools with rejection after rejection. Then I found this organization. I secured a job in Shanghai, but the government wouldn't issue a visa because of my age. So no job.

Back to square one, sort of.

I took the job with Mongolia even though others were pending, because it was a sure bet, and I'd already had one job turned down because the Chinese government (this particular province) wouldn't issue me a visa because of my age. *Over sixty,* I thought. Sometimes it wasn't always clear. I had a job pending in Thailand, which a friend wanted me to take only because she wanted to travel to Thailand.

I talked by phone to the recruiter from this international school in Mongolia and, when I accepted the job, I felt a weight had been lifted from my body. No lie!

Everything seemed perfect about the job in Mongolia. Experiencing a totally different culture. I didn't want to go to Europe or even South America. I really wanted a job in Asia. The salary and amenities seemed to click. I knew the weather was going to be a problem.

After accepting the position, and even before, I did a google search of Mongolia, Ulaanbaatar, the school, and anything else I could get my hands on. I knew I wasn't going to be in Kansas any longer. And again, I knew the weather would be a challenge. I was in contact with a few teachers from the school as well as the principal and got lots of info to help with the transition.

I remembered my first day at school, saying, "I'm back in the game."

It wasn't only having a job; it was having my own money again. Bringing in a paycheck. A brand-new life in an exotic place. I had a good feeling. I was going to be fine.

CHAPTER 25

Chris, The Aussie

I could safely say that my first two years in Mongolia would not have been the same without Chris, the Aussie. She was a flamingo—tall and full of color with a zest for life, a spirit moving through life like a bird in flight wings flapping for the next adventure.

We became best friends about halfway through our first year, partly because of one teacher who was a definite nemesis for both of us. A real pain in the butt, to put it mildly.

We loved our jobs teaching the Mongolian kids, but we found ourselves somewhat floundering, struggling because of this teacher. One day our principal called us into her office and, playing matchmaker, said, "You two would make a great team!"

Voila! We looked at each other, laughed, and a friendship began. We felt the power in numbers, but we tried to focus on the positive between us and outside of school.

Chris had worked at other international schools, but this was my first. So when I again felt discouraged with the behavior of that particular person, Chris introduced me to the saying, "International teachers fall under three categories: missionaries, misfits, or miscreants."

We had a good laugh, which I needed. But she seriously helped me, because I always struggled with whether people liked me no matter who or what they were. I wished it weren't so; I wished I could say opinions didn't matter, but it was not my story. So over the years, I shared this saying with other teachers. Some people didn't know what to say, but others got it right away, like my second-grade teacher partner, Christy.

Out of the mouths of babes.

When I got back to California, I told a friend about "missionaries, misfits, and miscreants." He laughed and asked, "Who and what are you?"

I didn't respond, but I stared at him with a twinkle in my eye, knowing who and what I was, the one who always took the road less traveled.

During 2009–2011, Chris taught fourth grade, and I had my first graders. Many times at our morning break, I visited her, and she always had wonderful insights as we shared a *cuppa* tea, as she called it, giving us the fortification to get us physically and mentally through the day.

We were buddies involving ourselves together in IWAM (International Women's Association of Mongolia), a group of women who did volunteer work to help orphans and other worthy causes. Once a month, they had a dinner meeting at some excellent restaurant. Chris and I joined at the same time, halfway through the first year.

We had book club, Bayraa (our chiropractor), and even Dawa, my driver. When we returned to our apartment complex after our weekly shopping spree, if there was snow/ice everywhere and it was freezing cold, Dawa helped us get our bags into the foyer. Then we had the long shlep up to the fourth floor, usually done in a couple of trips with lots of giggling, trying not to disturb others, but I am sure we did. Dorm life at the age of sixty-three!

One time we were in downtown UB in the dark with black ice still on the road as we tried to cross the street with cars zipping everywhere as we hung on to each other, laughing in between fear. It was a miracle we made it, but we always said, "The universe is with us!"

We found restaurants together, and lots of time through IWAM. She introduced me to her favorite Indian restaurant, and together we discovered a Korean restaurant that became another favorite. We sat on their patio in the fall and spring, enjoying the beautiful flowering trees. When I returned the second year, we went to Monet's, a five-star restaurant on the seventeenth floor of an office building overlooking the Square, to celebrate my sixty-fifth birthday. Of course, with a glass of wine!

During our second year, Chris got an apartment right next to me. When I was working on my novel, doing some hard editing, she would leave care packages at my door and then email me that I needed to check outside my door. What was friendship, if not that?

You need a friend when you are 6,100 miles away, in a foreign country, in a culture and people who are different from what you are used to, and a climate colder than hell.

On my last day, I remembered Dawa loading all my luggage in the car, and Chris walking down the stairs to join us. I was on my way to the airport, and she was going to an IWAM party. I waved to the school as Chris got in the car, so Dawa could drop her off for the party.

When she got out of the car, I rolled down my window, and we looked into each other's tearful eyes, and said, "I love you."

All these years later, we were still the best of friends. A year before COVID hit, I visited her and her daughter Kate in their beautiful Australia. When Chris met me at the airport, she didn't see me at first, so I walked up and said, "What are you doing here, shouldn't you be teaching those fourth graders in Mongolia?"

She laughed that Chris laugh as we hugged after eight years.

"Let's go have a cuppa," we said together.

CHAPTER 26

Dawa

Our lives were filled with players and plays—if we would only be.

When I first got to Mongolia, I became friends with Ondine, ESL coordinator at school, who was South African, but had lived for many years in Russia and now Mongolia. I was impressed with her because she spoke fluent Mongolian and Russian. She'd been living in Mongolia for a while, knew everyone, and had the answers to all our questions. Ondine was our "go to" person, right down to telling us that we really needed Dawa—maybe not when the weather was nice and warm, or even when it was a little cold, but when the REAL cold hit (minus 40F) with black ice, we sang his praises. And hers, of course!

What did I know about REAL cold? It was the start of fall, and the weather was still good; meaning no snow/ice; and I was able to walk about a mile down to Rosie's, the local 7-Eleven, the only market in 2009 to pick up some groceries in our area. But Ondine said, "You'll want to hire him and set up a weekly grocery shopping trip even though the weather is nice now. When the weather turns, you'll thank him!"

No truer words were ever spoken! In fact, it was the same line I used with Christy (my second-grade partner that third year in 2014). She immediately came on board for our weekly sojourn.

Dawa was a driver. That everyone had a driver sounded impressive to folks back home. It was hard to tell Dawa's age; but when I first met him, he was probably in his fifties. He spoke some English, and at times we both had trouble understanding each other. He was with me for the entire five years I was in Mongolia, and not merely for grocery shopping and lots of airport runs.

You know that last scene in *Out of Africa* when Meryl Streep was at the train station, saying goodbye to her right-hand man, knowing she would never see him again? That was me at the airport with Dawa in 2017. Except I cried more than Meryl did. We exchanged gifts. I gave him a seashell from the Pacific Ocean in California, and he gave me a box of chocolates. I watched his car drive off as I cried copious tears.

A fellow teacher was there who gave me a hug and said very softly, "It's hard."

It's always been hard for me to say goodbye, not only to people, but to places, homes—you name it. Letting go.

Beginnings were easier, but not endings. I liked the adventure of the start. Getting to know more of the world gave me a deeper understanding of myself.

Others felt there were no endings, just beginnings . . . that it was all a pause.

From an unknown writer: "We move to see new things."

Whenever I was in the car with Dawa, we always started out with the same conversations about the weather, traffic, and I asked him about his kids—two were at university (India and Japan). The younger son had attended a private Russian school in UB, and now he was going to university in Japan close to his sister. Occasionally now, something comes in on social media from either Dawa or his son, and I am transported back to another time.

Once we were done with our initial conversation, we pretty much sat in silence, which was awkward for me at first. But I learned over the years that Mongolians can sit for a long time without saying anything. Americans liked to chitchat—we like to "make busy." UB buses could be very crowded, but very quiet. In all the times I rode the bus to town, and even if it took forever, I never heard the Mongolians yell, "I've got to get home; what the hell is holding up this bus?"

Dawa and I had many experiences in the five years he drove me and others around UB. But one time we got caught in the worst traffic I ever encountered. Back home I was a road warrior and always compared everything to the 405 freeway in Southern California, the freeway that runs north and south through Los Angeles and LAX, where they kept adding lanes. The quote from *Field of Dreams*, "If you build it; they will come," came to mind.

So on this particular afternoon, we had left my friend Chris at the chiropractor's and was going to pick her up in an hour. I had a few errands to run not too far away. We started out inching our way into traffic and proceeded to inch our way to nowhere. In 2009, Mongolians were very creative drivers, driving up on sidewalks and anywhere there was a piece of land to advance forward. I was told by the Mongolians that most of them had never had formal training.

Back at the ranch, we continued to inch. Dawa ended up doing a circular turn and barely got back in time to pick up Chris, no errands, nothing.

But what really impressed me was that he never seemed flustered.

Even I held my tongue, which was unusual for me. I tried to crack jokes to keep myself at bay.

Mongolians were so stoic, living life as it came to them. Returning to the States, I had to get used to that attitude of "it should have happened yesterday," rats in a maze, running to and fro.

I often thought that maybe if nothing ever worked out in my life, I could return to UB and become a driver. At least, it wouldn't be as bad as the 405, right? And there would be Dawa.

CHAPTER 27

Goats and the Goat Herder

I had no choice except to watch the goats.

At the end of my first year, I moved from a second-floor apartment, staring at the school and the Zaisan monument that was lit up at night like a beacon to the fourth floor, facing the magnificent rolling hills. For a while, I was the only one up there, which earned me the name "the princess in the tower." Coined by my dear friend Chris, who at first said, "You're all alone up there!"

"But it gives me some privacy!" I responded, thinking that it also gave me some distance from the school, because at times many of us felt like rats in a cage with teachers working together *and* living together—reminiscence of dorm life from the sixties!

I almost always came home for lunch, which was a short distance from my classroom across the quad to the apartment stairs. Did I mention there were no elevators in these apartments?

Then I discovered the goats and the goat herder, and the moon.

Late in the afternoon, around 4:00, I left school and my first graders and headed to my apartment to make a cup of tea, have some yogurt and fruit, turn on my computer to check emails, accounts, and what was going on in the world.

Most of my emails came in the morning because of the fifteen to sixteen-hour time difference between California and Mongolia. After settling in to work on my novel, I looked out my apartment window to the hills silhouetted against the blue sky that was sometimes filled with ominous-looking clouds, and I watched and waited for the goats and the goat herder. What a far cry from my existence back home where my condo pretty much faced traffic and the only animals were people walking their dogs.

I remembered when I was ready to return home after two years, a friend said, "You're going to have trouble just staring at other condos and cars!" Now that I was home and typing at my computer with my desk facing a wall with a picture of me in the Gobi Desert, I wanted to turn my desk so it faced the window. But my friend was right; the view was not rolling hills, not the goats of UB, but instead the sounds and sights of the mailman's truck.

My principal, Kris, sometimes emailed me that the goats were coming over the ridge. Other times we emailed each other, "Did you see the goats today?"

Her apartment was on the second floor with a better angle to see them first. I was like my first graders when they anticipated recess. "Is it time, is it time?"

How many goats there were, I didn't know. A hundred possibly, maybe more. I tried counting, but one became two, three became one, the white and brown seemingly mixed with the black. What fascinated me was how they moved as one machine, covering the hills like a blanket over the crest, down through the tree line, and across the open slopes, eventually to their pens down in the valley close to where I lived. Even when the windows were open, I heard no sound, as if this were somehow a holy ritual only for a select few to witness.

Sometimes the goat herder was with them as they made this journey, and other times he went ahead, or it even appeared that no one was with them. But if I looked hard, I saw him at the bottom of the slope, waiting, ready to lead them back home.

Did he speak to them as you would little children? "You're safe with me now." Or was that my imagination? Or what I wanted to happen? Making up the fantasy was almost better than the reality.

I could never figure out their complete routine, but that was part of the thrill, the anticipation, the allure of it all. I usually did not see them going in the opposite direction over the hills to forage, because they left after I went to work. But when I did, it was just as exciting. And always a few stragglers, but that was why the dogs were there. But just as with the goats and the goat herder, I never heard a sound from the dogs.

I had started a definite relationship with the goat herder and his goats.

Was it possible that he knew, and/or they knew? My colorful imagination took off, making up stories that I kept to myself.

I could sit forever and watch them come over the hill, sometimes trying to decide where they might appear. They were like my magic little fairies dusting the hillside with their incredible speed, moving as one force. I strained my neck as the last one disappeared beyond my window. I laughed, "It's my own private movie. Where's the popcorn?"

When I was ready to leave Mongolia, I wanted to see the goat herder, but I never did. I was hesitant, a little shy, thinking language would be a barrier or maybe he wouldn't understand why I was saying goodbye. Would he think me strange that I found such joy in his goats, or would I be surprised?

It wasn't the first time I experienced the difference in cultures. My Mongolian friends told me, "We might seem to you that we are unfriendly at first. But it's merely our way.

Once we get to know you, you're family, and with us forever." That was an added reason I liked living in another country— to experience how they "took their tea."

Differences never scared me. In fact, I welcomed them. It was sameness that scared me. I didn't want to be trapped in a world of "vanilla."

We had big discussions about the comings and goings of the goats and their keeper as though the balance of world power was in our hands. "I think we need to see exactly where they live. Let's go down to where we think the pens are," suggested Chris.

"And what about the herder? Is it always the same man? Maybe it's a woman sometimes," replied Emily.

I thought about a woman herder; and of course, it could be. Mongolian women were very strong and worked as hard and maybe harder at many of the manual labor jobs that men did.

"Do you ever see the herder waiting for them at the bottom of the hill? He waits until several have crossed his path, and then he turns to walk down, letting the others follow. He never seems in a hurry," I said.

I found comfort in the fact that he didn't push time. I always pushed time as if I had the power to change it; I told six o'clock to hurry because seven was waiting.

We never went down to the pens, and we never saw the herder except from a distance. Was it enough that the goats brought us entertainment and something we had in common in a foreign place that at times seemed so alien? We were sometimes bonded by the strangest cords.

On my last day in Mongolia, right before leaving, they showed up. Were they saying goodbye? Why not? Wasn't the connection there? Why not believe the universe had conspired to give me one more moment, one more glance, one more.

The goats wandered as the children did on the hills and in the yard. A guide appeared for both as though a dinner bell had rung and they were to follow—some easier than others. Was there a sense of ritual that all knew instinctively? Was there an end, or was it simply a circle—or did either care about beginnings or endings? Was I the only one who got caught up in beginnings and endings?

When I returned to Mongolia after a few years, I looked for the goats and the goat herder from my apartment window, but was told they had moved the goats to another location because of new apartment buildings. I spent three more years in Mongolia and even on my last day, I still looked for those goats.

When I recently lived in Kauai, they used goats to "mow," and I watched them, remembering my Mongolian goats.

The moon was like the goats. It rose as a god over the same hills. The glowing round ball that had the strange face that could mesmerize. Was it a joke by another? Was it our keeper? The one who watched over us by night and sometimes by day. Was there a man in the moon? If so, did he try to speak to us, but we didn't hear? Too busy doing whatever it was we were doing.

Maybe silence was better, words coming when the story needed to be heard. Maybe that was the answer. Was the child still searching for the cross?

CHAPTER 28

Rear Window or Red Pajamas Guy

Part of my morning routine before going to work, besides having breakfast and going on the computer was to watch, from my fourth-floor apartment window, the activity in the gers on the other side of the fence. Red pajamas guy.

I called him that because most of the time that was what he wore. Red pajama-type bottoms. He varied the shirts and the outer gear, depending on the season and weather.

Like my routine, he also had one. Every morning I could count on him to first walk the well-worn path from his ger to the outhouse, which was about thirty feet away in the back. He walked with a slight limp. I thought maybe I felt a certain comradery with him because, during my second year, I also developed a slight limp. I thought it was from an injury—maybe something from yoga. After returning home in 2011, I discovered that I needed a hip replacement. When I had my successful surgery in 2012, I thought of him. I knew this kind of surgery wasn't an option for everyone. I knew I was lucky, because after my surgery, I was still able to go off and slay more dragons.

He had one of those dogs that was a mixture of various breeds and colors, who would walk faithfully with him, wait outside the outhouse door, and then make the walk back no matter what the weather was like. And during that first year, it became the coldest winter, known as *zud*, in thirty years, with temperatures well below zero and many times hovering around minus 30 and 40F. But they walked together, man and his dog, in the freezing cold and in the winter months in the morning darkness.

The dog slept outside and, depending on the weather, either lying up against the ger or in the doghouse. I sometimes felt sorry for the dog, but knew that was my Western culture coming through. Mongolians for the most part looked at all animals as working animals, not as pets. I saw dogs abused/kicked, but never from red PJ guy. I wasn't used to free-roaming dogs and, during my first weeks at school, I went walking with my friend Anna. Looking up at the nearby hills, I jumped and yelled, "See those dogs? What should we do?"

Anna shrugged her shoulders. Three large dogs, no leashes / no owners in sight, were on the hill not too far away from us, standing together like sentinels casually looking around. I felt scared, unsure, but Anna said, "Let's go . . . you'll be fine!"

I looked at her and then at the dogs, who seemed to be ignoring us. When we finally got far enough away, I pulled out my camera. The dogs acted like we weren't even there. At home, encountering a similar experience of free-roaming dogs could be a cause for alarm. However, I soon learned that most Mongolian dogs weren't on a leash and they left people alone. Packs of dogs roamed everywhere in UB. I was never afraid of dogs again, even when walking alone.

I never saw red PJ guy up close, even though on occasion when I went for a hike behind the school, around the gers, up into the hills, I peeked into the open-fenced area to see if I could see him. Curiosity is a strange thing.

I saw two gers; an extended family was very common in the Mongolian culture. They owned their ger, and the government provided the land for them to use. They weren't hooked up to the main heating for the city, so people burned everything, including trash (think incinerators in the fifties in LA), which became part of the very bad pollution problem.

But then again, keeping your child warm is a definite priority.

During the year that I was the "princess in the tower," the only person on the fourth floor, I watched red PJs and his interaction with other adults and kids. I was sure he was older—not the father, but rather the grandfather.

In the early fall, before the first light snow, he was always outside, sweeping the areas around the ger door and especially the path to the outhouse. His faithful dog by his side. I couldn't figure out how many people lived in those two gers, with all the comings and goings, but always there were children. He liked to carry the babies and play ball with the older kids. The toddlers enjoyed chasing the dog and falling down, as toddlers do all over the world. And like grandfathers all over the world, he was there to pick them up. I didn't understand what he was saying, but I envisioned something like, "Run, catch the ball. Be careful of your baby sister. Don't fall over the dog. Who wants to help Grandpa sweep the yard?" Words repeated all over the world. It made me both sad and happy—sad because I missed my grandkids, but happy to remember the same times I had with them.

Toward the end of fall, he prepared the gers for the cold, harsh, well-below-freezing winter by adding more layers; and in the spring those layers came off and repairs needed to be done. Sometimes he was alone, but other times women and men helped. Laughter mixed with the banging of hammers.

I was a faithful servant, watching and wondering. And just like the goats and the goat herder, at the end, I said my goodbyes through my fourth-floor window. After I left Mongolia, I wondered about red PJ guy, because I knew apartments were to be built on that site.

I was beginning to learn their importance of family.

When I returned for the second time in 2014, one thing I did was to look for him, but he was gone, and so were the gers. In its place were several unfinished apartment buildings that continued to sit like that for the next three years I was there.

Looking out from my second-floor apartment window, I thought about that old guy and his simple life, even though I knew it was harsh, but I was also envious of the simplicity and that everything he needed was right there. Was he still alive? And what about the dog? I knew I would never know. And he, along with the goats and the goat herder, would never know their importance in my life. It made me a little sad, especially as I once again looked out my condo window in Southern California to other condos, cars, and the sounds and sights of the mail truck.

CHAPTER 29

Millie's and Tom N Toms . . . Chez Away From Chez

Millie's was my chez away from chez. A mom-and-pop coffee shop owned by Daniel, who was Cuban, and his wife Densmaa, who was Mongolian. They met at university in Moscow. Their shop was written up in travel brochures and was a definite expat hangout. I occasionally went there with others, but I tried to save it as my own place of escape. My alone time, so to speak. Saturday mornings.

Although I loved my job and the people I worked with, but the idea that we basically lived and worked in such close proximity made it feel at times like we were rats in a maze. Unless something special was going on, like a birthday, or a movie, a special outing, I wanted my weekends to be for me. Lots of people activities occurred during the week, like IWAM (International Women's Association of Mongolia) where, besides helping others, we discovered the best restaurants and wines. And why not!

I also belonged to a book club, and sometimes the wine and cheese were more of the highlight than the book. Twice a month I volunteered at an English Club, helping primarily college-age students learn English and the American culture. We met Saturday mornings at a local coffee place. We had lots of interesting discussions. They loved America and followed US politics and major figures.

I needed my time to hike/walk, explore the city or just decompress. I had always been a people watcher, playing the director to the "actors" trying to figure out who and what people were, making up stories. I enjoyed chatting with strangers and getting to know the people who made each place special.

After going to Millie's for five years, when they saw me coming they knew what table I liked, my bottled water was opened and offered with a glass, and they had already started my favorite café mocha. The best in the world. I almost gagged when I returned to the States and tasted a Starbucks mocha for the first time in a long time—way too much sugar.

Before starting my breakfast, they always double-checked that I was still on for scrambled eggs, bacon, and toast. Daniel let me know that he always got the best eggs. Sometimes he joined me, and we talked about my family, his family, holiday times, and politics a few times.

Definitely like *Cheers*! I wanted people to know me, and I wanted to know them.

The other thing about Millie's was week after week I saw the same people, the same faces, but I never knew most of their names: the older British guy married to a Mongolian; the older Mongolian man who always, like me, came in alone. Some said hello, others didn't. Maybe a nod.

I am a combination of both my parents. My mother was very outgoing and liked to talk to everyone. If I was with her at the grocery store, the checker knew about my life and my kids' lives, divorces, you name it! For years, I was embarrassed that these strangers knew so much about me. But after my mother passed on, and as I got older, I appreciated that she passed on this ability to me to talk to almost anyone, anywhere. I wished I could tell her "thank you." But I was caught up in what irritated me, so I didn't see the forest for the trees.

The opposite was my father who was not a people person and who lost himself in books and the ocean. From him I learned to appreciate being alone, to read, and enjoy the simple things of life. He could sit for hours staring at the ocean, sometimes with his binoculars and other times not. I could go to a restaurant or coffeehouse and be contented to watch the world go by. Why is it we understood our parents after they are gone?

Friday afternoon rolled around, and we were ready to leave school for the day right at 3:20, when the kids left. I packed up my belongings and, if the weather was good, I walked down to Tom N Toms coffee place about a mile away. If the weather wasn't good, sometimes I called for a taxi to take me back and forth. I needed my break. I needed my time to sit, enjoy my latte or mocha, and watch the world go by. I could sit for hours. Thanks, Dad! It was as though I was watching a movie. Better. The old truck with the horses tied up in the back. Why didn't they fall out? Cows wandering into the parking lot. Impatient drivers sometimes honking their horns at cows, people, and cars. If the weather was good in late spring, the fountain across the street was spewing water in the air, and little kids enjoyed the water breeze. Parents took pictures with cellphones. Barbecues were smoking. People were walking. Sometimes I saw students I knew either from my class or from school, and they were always so cute when they saw me, coming up and saying, "Hi, Ms. Diane." Looking surprised that I was anywhere but school. I miss that.

I always reminded the servers how I wanted my hot drinks—really hot, but usually if it was someone who knew me, they interrupted, saying, "Yes, we know 'very hot' and also in a to go cup." We had a good laugh. That *Cheers* feeling again.

When I left these places for the last time to return to the States, I didn't cry as I did with Dawa; but a sadness came over me. That last day from Millie's, I walked back to my apartment, each step taking me further away physically as well as emotionally, but searing memories in my heart. Not long ago, I vowed to a fellow teacher from Mongolia that I would return to the "Land of the Blue Sky."

My heart knew, even if I didn't always.

CHAPTER 30

Leaving Home

I remembered the night I left, or should I say, early in the morning. One of those early morning flights going into Asia. I waited downstairs in my condo with two very large suitcases and one medium sized, both for check-in, and two carry-on computer-type bags and a purse. After doing a fair amount of overseas traveling, I thought I had downsized. But in the next several years, I learned to take even less.

I was leaving my condo empty/not renting it out, and my neighbor friend was looking after it, taking in mail, making sure water didn't flood the upstairs and make its way down-stairs. I knew I was fortunate to have her. I said goodbye to family and friends including my two-and-a-half-year-old grandson. I checked everything off that list that had be-come an entity on its own. "A list for the list," my nephew and I joked.

I was alone, alone in my own thoughts. I paced.

Garage door up, waiting for the van. Sigh of relief when I saw his headlights coming into the driveway.

I'll never forget the feeling as the driver loaded up my suitcases, and I looked around my condo and blew a kiss, like I was saying goodbye to a lover. "I'll see you in ten or eleven months; be good." I wasn't coming home for the holidays. I'd already made plans to go to Hong Kong and Thailand for Christmas break.

The garage door went down, and I climbed into the van with an ache in my heart.

But I didn't realize something else at the time. Many months and even years down the road, I recognized that something else like hope had always been with me.

I was flying LAX to Beijing to Ulaanbaatar, Mongolia. The flights were long, and the time difference was even longer.

Beijing Airport was a nightmare. No help about how to transfer to MIAT, the Mongolian Airlines that would take me to my final destination. One person said that I would have to leave the main airport. Very confusing. I saw myself stranded in China with no visa and missing my flight to Mongolia. But alas, the universe stepped in, because I ended up with some people from our own government who figured out our flights to Ulaanbaatar.

Relief. Well, relief after we had dinner and then actually boarded our flight. I did get on, but initially wasn't sure if MIAT was going to let me board with my two rather large carry-ons and purse. I remembered just marching through. I don't like to think of myself as the "Ugly American," but well, one does what one has to do.

The best feeling in the world when traveling was getting to the destination and seeing a friendly face or a sign with your name on it. One time I flew to Nairobi, Africa, to go on a safari. It was my first time in Africa, and I had arrived at 4:00 a.m. As I walked out of Customs, I prayed that someone was there to pick me up. And what would I have done if they weren't?

But sure enough, a sign with my name on it!

I'd been in touch with the school principal, Kris, and her husband, Mr. Chris, as I call him even to this day. Kris said she'd be at the Chinggis Khan Airport when we arrived very late at night. After I went through customs, I walked out into a sea of people, and there she was, waving at me and embracing me with a big hug, like I was family. We left in the school van and, as we were driving, I tried like a little kid to take in as much as I could.

My apartment was right across from the principal's apartment. Maybe it was the expression on my face when I walked in that made her say, "You can make it your own, decorate it anyway you want." I didn't want to disappoint her, so I smiled.

The shades were up, and I had a view of the school, but what I really liked was the view of Zaisan monument on the hill, rising like a monolith up into the sky, all lit up.

The gods must have been with me because I hardly got any sleep that night, trying to "make it my own" as my principal suggested. The first thing I did was set up my computer so I could email my sons and friends to let them know I was okay. Somehow I got on Skype, and my son was also on. It felt wonderful to connect with him since I was so far from home.

I had a one-bedroom with a bathroom, living room, and a very small kitchen. The kitchen reminded me of when I was little and played house with my dolls. Everything was miniature. The stove looked like a Playskool stove or something for Barbie, with two electrical burners; and the refrigerator was a little bigger than a hotel minibar. Very much like what you would find in Europe. The tiny freezer was inside the refrigerator, which accumulated ice almost faster than the snow outside. Then there was the bathroom with all the pipes exposed. I liked that the bathtub was big, even though it was awkward to climb in and out. It had a handheld shower, which I learned to love. After five years, I missed it when I returned to California. I took a deep breath, realizing that I came from a society where bigger was better: cars, TV, homes, appliances, etc. I vowed to make this work, enjoy the experience, and not be the Ugly American.

In those first two years, the only time I panicked was when at 3:00 a.m., I woke to water streaming down my walls from the laundry room upstairs. I was pretty sure I caused the whole floor, maybe the whole building, to wake up, including my principal who, with her experience working in other countries, was used to this.

To say I went through a metamorphosis like a butterfly in all the five years I was in Mongolia is an understatement. I went from panicking when the internet went down to just taking it all in stride and helping newbies to relax. I became Mongolian.

I loved that first day where Mr. Chris took us around to the grocery stores. We walked to the bar/restaurant/little store, which eventually got the name "scary store." I thought that name stuck because one time we walked in, and electrical wires were laying all over the floor. We then went on to Rosie's Market, which became home-away-from-home for the next two years. And of course, we stopped at Cozy Nomads Restaurant. There wasn't much more those first two years.

I discovered the ger camp above Cozy's and walked/hiked up the road into Bogd Khan, the sacred mountain (where I saw my first two-humped camel, a Bactrian).

Everything was open—no apartments; I could see for miles. Sometimes on a Sunday I hiked behind the school up to where the Buddhist retreat was and have my lunch. That all started to change during the second year, with new apartments being built. And when I returned three years later, it had changed drastically. I could barely see the retreat through the construction.

On full-moon nights, I laid on my bed with the blinds open, watching as that moon rose big and bold. It slowly made its ascent, rising to the top of the mountain and beyond. I watched the flow as it ascended, creeping ever-so-slowly to the top of the mountain, and finally bursting forth and rising higher and higher like it was a puppet on a string. On my last night in Mongolia, I asked myself if I'd ever have that feeling again. When I lived in Cambodia, I looked for the moon, and again in Kauai and Italy, and all the places in between. I had driven on the Interstate 5 in Southern California and looked up and saw that big moon take over the sky, even in a busy metropolis.

I was walking up from Rosie's back to the apartment complex—about a mile or so in the cold. Being born in New Jersey and living there until I was almost eight years old, I only remembered the cold from a child's mind. Mud rooms where my mother helped me out of my snowsuit. The sky turning black because a snowstorm was coming. It wasn't until my family moved to Southern California, and my dad took us up to the mountains, that the cold seeped into my feet and hands and hurt. My dad carried us to the car, because we were all in so much pain.

But I was getting older. Walking up from Rosie's, no one was there to carry me.

Then a car pulled up—teachers ready to give me a ride as I walked with my head down against the wind. I was wrapped up like a mummy, only my eyes showing, but I felt that bitter cold even so. They encouraged me to get in, saying, "Don't you know it's dangerous walking where it's below zero?"

They were right, of course. What was I thinking? I wasn't; still a Southern California novice. We all knew people who had gotten frostbite.

I got in the car.

The entire time I was in Mongolia, I kept every part of me warm except for my hands, and I never did have total success even wearing two set of gloves. But I had my Uggs, and I had my Russian fur hat.

Wasn't I good to go!

CHAPTER 31

Year of Firsts

If you live in America, well for me, specifically Southern California, you might experience an electrical outage every few years due to who knew what. They never told us why or what had happened as we stood outside our home, kibitzing with neighbors, speculating on what had happened. But it was a terrific way to introduce yourself, get to know your neighbors, especially since in my area, people seemed to keep to themselves. A foreign concept to Mongolians who sometimes had trouble understanding why I sometimes wanted to eat alone or drink coffee by myself. I discovered this concept of family in other countries like East Timor and Cambodia, and even in Kauai, a part of America, but not just geographically separate, but separate in the concept of family. When I lived in Kauai, I discovered they had a word for family, *ohana*, which was based on something universal: family that you become a part of.

So back in Southern California, along with the electricity, you might also experience your cable company having problems, which meant you lose internet or TV for maybe a few hours or, God forbid, an afternoon.

But I can't ever remember the water/sewage line exploding and having to get water from the market down the street to flush the toilet or, better yet, no flush and no running water! In 2009 I was three days into Mongolia when that happened in our apartment complex for a day! It was still summer, and still hot! But there I was emptying big water bottles into the toilet. And sometimes we couldn't even do that. Yeah, let your imagination go wild!

For others, this wasn't their first time going through something like this, but it was for me—the new kid on the block. I was blessed or cursed that I don't have a very good sense of smell. Suffice to say, ever since I could remember, I couldn't smell.

A blessing in this case.

I am the first to admit that I was spoiled with all we have in America. I had certainly taken it for granted and could barely put up with cable being down, or any other minor irritants. And I was not very patient. What was I going to do when I couldn't retrieve my email or surf the net?

When I first experienced the internet not working in my apartment, I immediately went to my principal's apartment, which was across from mine. Lucky her.

"It'll come back on, don't worry," Kris said. "It's Mongolia."

"It's Mongolia," became a mantra for a lot of us, including the Mongolians. It certainly helped to transition me into "being Mongolian," being something beyond myself. I discovered later on how very patient my principal had been with the new kid on the block.

"Don't drink the water" was one of the first rules I learned when I got to UB. I had traveled to several developing countries, so I was used to this, but traveling and "living" were not the same thing. We bought bottled water, plus each floor had a water treatment machine, well except at the end of my first year when I moved to the other side, which was considered the Mongolian side because mostly Mongolians lived there and they just drank the water—no treatment machines. So I had to walk down four flights of stairs, fill up my water bottles, and shlep once again up to the fourth floor. (I mentioned there were no elevators in the apartment complex.) Other buildings in town, like State Department Store, had elevators, but not us.

But hell, it was worth the shlepping to see those goats and the moon rising so majestically over those hills!

Communal washers, but no dryers. Hanging my laundry all over my apartment, including on the heater pipes. Ah! The heater pipes. We had no control on when they turned on or off. The pipes were regulated by the government, and sometimes they were still on even when the weather started getting hotter outside! Believe me, I tried everything to turn off those babes! It was a comedy watching all of us try to adjust the knobs, to either lower or turn off completely, but really to no avail.

We didn't have COVID, but we had a swine flu scare that first year in 2009, and school was closed for six weeks right after fall break. We opened one week before Christmas break in December.

I learned a lot of patience in Mongolia. What else was I going to do? Getting things fixed or done meant being patient—not my long suit. But I was bound and determined to be like them. Even if I couldn't speak the language, I would become Mongolian, embracing the culture, the people, and the land. Again, it didn't take me long to start using the phrase, "It's Mongolia," as much as the Mongolians and other expats used it.

This was my place, and I wanted to become a part of it. I needed to be a part of it. Something inside me cried out for this. Did it start when I was five, living in New Jersey, and in the playground sand I said to myself and others, "I'm digging to China."

A lot had been written about "digging to China," many theories. But for me it was always something beyond the moment, beyond the place.

At five years old, I didn't understand this, but now I knew it was there. For others, maybe it was no big deal, but was it the beginning of my wanderlust? Wanderlust that is still with me even today.

CHAPTER 32

Expats

"Travel–to taste and see a different way of life. To experience everyday things for the very first time. To wander roads in a foreign place for no purpose at all but to taste a way of life outside of my own."

— source unknown

Why did I like doing the expat thing—teaching and living in another country? The adventure. It was always the adventure. And it was always the excitement of new beginnings, of being a gypsy, something different; not to simply travel, but living the life of another culture, people, and land, experiencing. The simplicity, the freedom of not keeping up with the Joneses. As if the pressure was off.

Being a seven-year-old again before knowing about life.

I talked with a lot of expats, and they all agreed with my analogies; plus, if they had kids, they wanted to raise their kids in an international setting, so they would know more about the world. My principal from those first two years had the best story. Kris said, "We met when he was a lawyer, and I was a bartender. We got into teaching because we wanted to live and work overseas and not in the States. Our first stop was Bangkok with two small children, and we never looked back. We've been doing this for twenty-plus years."

Recently, I spoke with her, and she said they were never going to retire! And I knew for a fact that they had known a few harrowing experiences, as all of us expats had.

My kind of people!

I was a geographer, so I knew the importance of place and finding your place. And I had my place in Mongolia.

That was what all of us were searching for, even if we didn't understand that "place" was what it was. To belong, to have our clan, our people. Endless books have been written on this subject. In the beginning of time, our ancestors knew this. Some of us find a mate, start a family, and many times have an extended family. We find a home in an area that suits us. A job. A career. Purpose.

Mongolia gave me purpose. The expat friendships that I developed and nurtured, I still maintain after all these years. A common thread ties us together. And when you don't have a common thread, you feel displaced, "out of sorts" some called it.

I was searching again after leaving my teaching position in Phnom Penh, Cambodia, because of COVID. More recently, I spent eight months on the beautiful island of Kauai, and now I was back in the charming coastal town of San Clemente, California.

This quote says it all: "I will not let the fires consume me; instead I will rise as a phoenix out of the ash!"

CHAPTER 33

Horses and Soldiers

Mongolian State Honor Guard at Chinggis Khan Square in Ulaanbaatar

Not the changing of the guard at Buckingham Palace, but this was just as exciting, with pomp and circumstance and colorful costumes. Just as regal. Thunderous music filled the air, and I could almost picture Chinggis Khan with his loyal soldiers riding across the plains of Eurasia, conquering all in their path.

Every Saturday, if weather permitted, the Mongolian State Honor Guard, a unit of the Armed Forces of Mongolia, performed their ceremony at Chinggis Khan Square in downtown UB. Marching in step, proudly holding their

Chinggis Khan Square

weapons in front of Chinggis Khan's statue. The statue is formidable, massive. I sensed the Khan's presence still guarding the Square, which had been built in Russian style with a vast plaza surrounded by some of UB's historic landmarks.

Mongolians are a proud people, understanding the importance of history and heritage. The soldiers wore boots with the toes turned up to respect the earth by not digging into the soil. The toes made ambiguous footprints so your enemies cannot tell what direction you are headed. No left or right feet, they were made the same; and as you wore them, they conformed to your feet. Buddhists felt this type of boot covered less ground, and fewer bugs and worms are killed with each step.

Chinggis Khan's soldiers began riding at an early age, and hunting as soon as they could hold a bow. Mongol horses and people were tough, agile, and sturdy, with great endurance.

I stayed with a friend at the pristine Lake Khuvsgul located at the northern border of Mongolia, and we rode these horses. The lake was the largest fresh water lake in Mongolia by volume and second largest by area, and close to the southern end of Lake Baikal in Russia, considered the deepest lake in the world. The surface of the lake froze over completely in winter but, because it was fall, the only snow was on the mountain ranges surrounding us, offering a breathtaking view. Our ger was just a few yards from the lake, and owned by Grandma who was always very friendly and warm.

As we mounted the horses, we were scared to be honest, because we were told by the guide that, unlike our horses back home, these horses were not pets. He warned, "Don't have anything dangling and/or make any sudden moves, because they could bite!"

We looked at each other and for a split second wondered why we were doing this. I was handed the reins, and at that moment the horse decided to buck and take off! My eyes must have been as big as saucers as the guide quickly grabbed the reins and steadied the horse. I swore I heard a chuckle.

But I didn't get off, and neither did my friend. I sometimes cursed my sense of adventure.

Horses in Eastern Mongolia

Once we relaxed and had nothing dangling, the ride around the lake was breathtaking. We were there in the off-season, so we had the crystal blue lake, the guide, and the horses to ourselves: snow-capped mountains, no sounds except the sounds of contentment.

Later in the day as we sat at the lake, we heard the throat singers as they played their horsehead fiddles, and we thought we were in paradise.

In throat singing, the performer produces a fundamental pitch and simultaneously one or more pitches over that. Many male herders could throat sing, but women had begun to practice the technique as well. The singer identified the spirituality of objects in nature, not merely in their shape or location, but in their sound as well. Human mimicry of nature's sounds was seen as the root of throat singing.

As I enjoyed the moment, I thought back on the ceremony at the Square and the spirit of those young soldiers, even though they probably would never have to fight the fight their ancestors had.

I wondered about the horses of Lake Khuvsgul, my own life since "digging to China," and a novel, *The Good Earth,* by Pearl S. Buck that described life in a Chinese village. I came across this book as a young girl; and it was another catalyst for me wanting to travel to exotic places.

Lost in memories, I drifted back to the singing and what made me love Mongolia.

CHAPTER 34

Taxis and Hitchhiking

Waving for a Taxi Downtown

Dodging traffic. I was not used to cars not stopping for pedestrians: part of becoming Mongolian, I learned, dodging cars to make it across the road.

In 2009 it was every woman for herself. When I returned a few years later, some intersections had designated crosswalks even with green and red pedestrian signals. However, drivers didn't always observe the "rules" and, for that matter, neither did pedestrians. Old patterns are hard to change.

Sometimes I felt my head spinning, as though I was Linda Blair in *The Exorcist*.

Mongolians and expats who had lived here for some time said, "Just go! Walk with the Mongolians. You're like rocks in a river. The cars will go around you!"

"Okay," I whispered sheepishly to myself. I imagined getting slammed from a 4,000-pound car. But eventually that mantra became my mantra, sort of like a cat-and-mouse game, wondering who was the cat and who was the mouse.

My girlfriend visited that second year, and I had to drag her across the street, trying not to look at the fear in her face, while I was thinking, *This is normal.*

Yes, I was becoming Mongolian, just as my Mongolian friends said!

I didn't even hitchhike when I was younger, growing up in a Mayberry-type town, USA, where I pretty much never thought of rapists and pedophiles (my family did warn against getting in a stranger's car). But there I was, for all practical purposes, hitchhiking in a foreign country. Could that be even worse? Most of the teachers didn't have cars, so we either walked or took buses or taxis. *I was not using my thumb*, I told myself, but waving my hand, flapping it up and down, like I had wings and not hands, facing traffic, hoping a car would pull over to take me home or to my next destination in UB.

We got really good at knowing what cars would possibly stop—older cars, a little beat up, and usually with a single, male driver. Oh! And white, lots of white cars. Never families, and on a rare occasion, a woman. Of course I didn't just start to do this without some guidance from those who came before me, like Ondine, our "go to" person. She knew the language and customs. I was impressed, and we were all lucky.

"Don't be out alone at night, flagging down a taxi!" she added to the instructions.

"Yep!" I said, wanting to follow orders.

Was my mother turning over in her grave? I imagined friends and family back home shaking their heads.

I was downtown on my way back to my apartment and, as I was flapping my hand, someone tapped me on my shoulder. I turned, and this older guy pointed to his older, white four-door Nissan Sentra (the typical taxi car), and I knew that meant he would give me a ride.

The more I lived in Mongolia, the more I understood the phrase, "When in Rome . . . " I got in and spoke what I called Mongolian "taxi language"—*chigeeree* (straight), *baruun* (right), *zuun* (left), and of course, the magic word *Zaisan*. He shook his head in an affirmative motion, and I knew I was fine. Suffice to say, there was always lots of pointing and arms waving.

After five years in Mongolia, I was embarrassed to admit that was pretty much the extent of learning the language. I did know *sain baina uu* (hello) and *bayarlala* (thank you). I was never very good with foreign languages. I didn't have an ear and, for me, Mongolian with his guttural sounds was like trying to learn French, which I failed at miserably before I went on an extensive European trip with my second husband.

Another time, I got into this old guy's car, and he asked, "Are you American? How long have you been here?"

When I said, "Almost two years," he laughed with a twinkle in his eye and replied, "Let me teach you some other Mongolian words! You need to learn more."

I explained to him that I wasn't very good with languages, but he was relentless. Being a teacher, I understood the concept. We shared a laugh, and I told him he was a good teacher and when I left his car, he said, "Enjoy your time here."

I still left him with the same taxi language.

I took a wrong bus one day as I was trying to get back to my apartment from the center of town. It was during my first two years, and I panicked because very few people spoke or even understood English, so I knew I was on my own.

I was such a novice back then! Over time, I learned that you really can't get "lost" in UB—it isn't that big!

But I finally got off the bus and started walking back, looking for a taxi or some guy driving alone who I knew would stop. Eventually, I saw a guy parked on the side of the road and went up to him sitting in his car and asked if he was a taxi. He nodded his head *yes* and off we were back to school and apartment. Was I crazy or what? Maybe I wasn't such a novice! And just maybe I liked pushing the envelope, doing things I'd never do at home. Was there something freeing in this life I was leading? I thought so; I knew so.

When I returned to Mongolia after being home in Southern California for almost three years, UB had become more sophisticated with more "regular" taxi companies, some based out of Korea. New, black, clean cars looked like NYC. The school encouraged us to use those taxis instead of "flagging down." They were a phone call away, and for the most part dependable, albeit costlier.

After a while, they got to know me; even if they had trouble with English, they knew where I wanted to go. On Saturday mornings, it was usually Millie's Restaurant, my "chez away from chez." When I started to tell them, the driver would say with a smile, "Yes, I know, Millie's."

It was nice to be known.

When the weather was really bad, with all that ice and snow, they were a lifesaver. A must for me because, even in five years, I never did get very good balancing on that ice. Not like the Mongolian women who walked on black ice, wearing three-inch heels!

Usually on Saturdays, if the weather permitted, I took the bus into town and a taxi home. The buses from Zaisan to downtown were empty, but returning they were always packed, and there was the occasional pickpocket. I never felt in danger in UB, but if I went out at night, it was always with a crowd. I remembered what Ondine had said.

On this particular night, we had gone to a Trivia game way across town and, while we were inside, it snowed a lot!

Jacob said, "We need to flag down a taxi."

"Can we call a taxi?" I asked, not wanting to venture far into the snow.

"It'll take too long at this time of night and with the snow," was the response. I moaned, walking like a slow duck so I wouldn't fall.

We ended up trying to jam five people into a taxi. Everyone was laughing except the driver, who somehow conveyed that it was against the law to have more than four in a taxi, and he could get a ticket. "Really?" We all said at once looking from one to another. This was news to us.

Sometimes rules were made up along the way. We split up the team and everyone was happy.

I always liked a challenge and in 1963, when I got accepted to San Francisco State, I didn't have housing. My parents put my brother and me, he was fourteen and I was seventeen, on a plane to go to SF State. We had to figure out transportation from the airport to the college, and find housing in someone's home. We did all of this via buses and taxis. And no internet! A wing and a prayer! So maybe figuring out how to get around UB was in my DNA.

Mongolians always asked me, "How do you like our country? What do you like the most? America is very different, isn't it?"

Although I knew some of my students and several parents had been to America, most Mongolians I met had never been outside UB or the countryside.

Walking home one day, I took in my surroundings of broken sidewalks, old Russian block buildings, the gers interspersed with the new construction of glass buildings, and I said to myself, "This still feels more like home than home." That comfortable feeling again; but more than comfortable, I belonged. A feeling that stays with me even to this day.

CHAPTER 35

Clouds

How could a sky be threatening and soothing at the same time? Was it only me? When the clouds came, they came with a sort of vengeance, rolling across the cerulean-blue sky like the Mongolian horses that rode across the yellow grassy plains. They came with a purpose it seemed, almost angry in their intensity.

Why did I like it? Why was I captivated (because I was)— my eyes tracking the movement that was hypnotic, relaxing? Shapes didn't stay for long, but moved quickly on to maybe another purpose. Nothing like that mystery back home in Southern California.

I saw the same clouds when I lived in Cambodia and Kauai: cumulus, puffy, cotton-like, fluffy, piled up in a heap. But those places were tropical. Mongolia was not tropical.

Mongolia was known as the land of the blue sky. The landscapes were wide, and I could see far out to the horizon, deepening the experience of seeing blue sky all around. As if the sky might engulf even me if it had its way, or if I let it.

Did I have that power? Or did it?

Above the school was the mountainous region called Bogd Khan, a protected area considered to be holy and sacred by shamans and Buddhists. Was there something about this mountain? What did it know? I suspected the clouds were a part of this holiness.

When I was at college in San Francisco, I walked to the ocean from San Francisco State and strolled along the beach that was usually void of people. My best memories were when the ocean was gray and the waves were pounding—fierce and angry, but somehow soothing. I had no desire to swim in that ocean; but like the Mongolian sky, it gave me comfort.

As I traveled the world, I looked up at the sky, wondering not only what it could give me, but what I could give in return. What was it asking of me? Because I knew it was. Maybe that time thing again when I needed to be in the moment because, as we had all learn, those moments are fleeting.

Even now I miss the show that the Mongolian cloud angels performed. It made me think of my sister, and that I wanted to write her a letter so we could laugh once again about Outer Mongolia. It was a joke when we were kids that, if you did something bad, you could be sent to Outer Mongolia.

Little did I know.

I could write the letter, but there was no one to send it to; my sister had passed a while back, right after I returned.

CHAPTER 36

Rainbows

"What is it about rainbows?" I asked no one in particular.

When I first moved to UB in 2009, the hills were alive, not with the sound of music, but with a peaceful serenity that came from not having hordes of people and hordes of structures taking up space. So when the rains came, and then the sun, I could look out my apartment window toward those hills and usually catch a rainbow. That magical force nature created almost defied logic, at least for me.

Like a little kid, I always hoped to see the beginning and the end, wishing in those childish ways that a pot of gold was at the end, guarded by those sometimes scary, but always mischievous, leprechauns, and their fairy friends.

If it was childish, why not? And who cared? Could I capture one of those leprechauns and have it grant me three wishes for its freedom and mine?

Over the five years I spent in Mongolia, not only the hills, but everything about this country became a magical place for me so different from where I lived in Southern California. And when I left permanently to return "home," I sometimes felt that magic stayed behind. And even now, like a feather, it tickles me with whispers in my ear to return.

I knew in my heart I would return some day; maybe not in the capacity of teaching like I had, but I would return. In Isak Dinesen's book, *Out of Africa*, she spent many years in

East Africa; but once she left, she never returned. I didn't want that to be me.

More recently, after leaving Cambodia because of COVID-19, I had the same feeling, that magic didn't follow me back home. I found myself more comfortable in developing countries with the people who lived there than at home. I knew other expats who had lived and worked overseas felt the same way. Even if they didn't say it in so many words, I saw it in their eyes.

I wanted to feel that magic again. It couldn't just vanish from my life. I wanted those mischievous leprechauns to entice me with pots of gold, with wishes.

Weren't there still dreams to be experienced and hills sprinkled with gold dust not yet explored? Mysterious woods, enchanting gardens, and unknown temples. Magic, dreams, freedom. Again I asked, "What is it about rainbows?"

CHAPTER 37

Into the White

Snow Drifts at My Apartment

Right outside my apartment window, not much to look at, but it was the only plant in the stark white snow that looked like a soothing blanket, but I knew better.

Not a tree, not a forest, not the woods that I loved.

But this plant was different, or was it? No leaves, stick-like, maybe no hope. But still reaching up to the sun that would shine almost every day, 257 days recorded, even when temperatures were well below zero. There was no warmth, but I thought the plant had patience. I wanted it to survive, just like I wanted to survive.

My imagination kicked into high gear, and I envisioned a kind of fairy tale home beneath the cold, with a door and windows that glowed yellow with inviting warmth.

They say all good things came to those who wait. But patience is not my long suit.

The cold was so cold that it hurt to breathe as I stepped out first from one door into the antechamber and then finally out into the harsh, minus 40F cold. The sun was shining, how deceiving because there was no warmth from that round, yellowish orange ball. The sky was a blazing blue. There was something different about the skies in Mongolia versus the skies in California. In Mongolia, I always thought the skies were yelling to be heard: they were fierce, scary like "big sky" Montana. Or almost like the ocean when a storm was brewing.

When I was at San Francisco State, I loved to walk down to the ocean because most of the time it was a gray swirl of choppy waves that you thought should be scary, but were actually very comforting for me. That was how I felt about the Mongolian sky. They had something to say, especially as the cumulus clouds moved swiftly across them. I almost felt or sensed or even saw the curvature of the earth as opposed to Southern California where it seemed so vanilla, so tame, so boring.

The last dirty snow had been shoveled away, and the temps were rising. I never thought I'd say this, and we all said it, "Once the temps hit zero or slightly above zero (could have been plus 5F), we thought we were having a heat wave." Time to venture outside, and not only with Dawa, but time to wander the streets of UB and do some walking.

I asked myself why I was here. The question always seemed to be looming—why was I here? But I didn't always sit for the answer. Did it matter? Would the outcome be any different? Maybe I didn't recognize the answer. Did the answer come, maybe not in the form I was seeking?

It felt as if the white was here to stay—like me. The white of the snow was here to stay until it turned a dirty black, and still I stayed. Did I have a choice? Did any of us? We each had that which we needed to accomplish. Maybe some did, and some didn't.

The snow was pristine at first as it fell from the sky, dusting the ground, clinging to the delicate limbs like flour. But I noticed as time went on, the white became dark, black, as though anticipating its own death.

I thought I knew how that plant felt. But did I? When I had to venture out into the stark white, I made sure I had all the essential items: coat, hat, scarf, and mittens. But that plant had nothing, and yet I knew it would survive into the spring, summer, and fall; sprout leaves; but then once again be alone in the white. That was what Mongolia was all about. For the flora and fauna, and for the humans as well. Extreme.

I was sometimes alone in the white. When you lived as an expat in Mongolia (I was told), you better be comfortable with yourself. You better like being alone. Because with the bitter cold months, you could spend a lot of time inside, a lot of time by yourself. You better like books.

The softness of the white was deceiving. I knew it; I had learned that through trial and error. I remembered my first snow in Mongolia—the excitement of something different, new, foreign to my Southern California eyes and body. A different sensation felt by all senses.

Playing in it with my first graders with all their innocence, and mine.

By the time six months rolled around, the beautiful white powder that had looked so soft and enticing at one time became black, dirty, and ugly to look at. Stained yellow from human and animal urine. Not to mention the black ice that sometimes formed under the snow where one slip could leave you with a one-way ticket home. I was done with it. Almost didn't return for a second year. Almost didn't finish my first year!

But the universe stayed with me, comforted me even through the lack of color, no flowers, only the white, black, and gray.

I seriously thought about leaving permanently, going back home after eight months, but then my principal stepped in, "Go now for a week!"

So at Easter break, I hopped on a plane for home. I remembered my excitement at seeing the coastline as we made our way down from the Northwest into California and then landing at LAX. I rented a car and drove down to the beach. Seeing the blue of the Pacific for the first time in eight months, I started to cry as I called my friends. I only had a few days so I saw a few family, and friends, which was all I needed. I was fine. More than fine. When I got back to UB, I was ready to continue the journey that I started and not merely continue, but delight in it. Who would have thought?

As I returned, I was greeted by friends and teachers welcoming me back, like the warrior I knew I was becoming. The person I've always been, but didn't know it.

Like that plant always seeking the warmth, hope against hope, but eventually with patience finding the sun. I thought I discovered what it meant to be Mongolian. What it meant to be true to me. To be me.

They said all good things came to those who wait.

CHAPTER 38

Getting Back on the Horse

I'd been working on my novel for the last six years—editing, editing, and more editing. If you are a writer, you understood what I am talking about. I was happy with the first one hundred pages, but then it hit—the all-consuming writer's block. So I emailed my writing coach, who gave me the much-needed permission to put the novel aside. "Don't forget it," he said, "but you need to be writing more than one thing. Write what you want, no anxiety about form, editing—just write what you want to write. Something will appear. You'll surprise yourself."

I hit the keys. So far I was not surprised. Sometimes the anxiety crept in like a robber in the night, threatening to take it all. I knew it helped to fantasize a story and write about it. I was good at fantasy. I started pecking away.

"I'm in this little café in a small village in Italy with my laptop. A cappuccino warms my hand. People are coming and going. One other person sits in the corner— an old man sipping his espresso . . . well, old men don't sip their espresso. He'll move on, I'm sure, to something stronger soon, very soon. You can do that in Italy. He nods his head at me, but we never talk. Oh! He knows all about me—the older American writer. *Why is she here?*

She wonders herself, but the food and drink are so good. The ambience incredible. She thinks maybe she can tell stories about travel, be a mental traveler like Isak Dinesen in *Out of Africa*."

I realized something had happened to me. It was like a genie waving a magic wand as I found myself writing arbitrary one-liners, which progressed into the two years I spent in Mongolia. I had so many experiences and, at times when I thought about them, they acted like little children grabbing my apron strings, all wanting attention, all wanting to be heard.

So I took a deep breath and then took them one at a time and started to write about the hills with the wandering goats and the ever-present goat herder, the rising moon, the old man who lived with his family in a ger right beyond the fenced in area of my apartment complex, taking his morning walk to the outhouse (even in the snow) with his faithful dog beside him. He walked with a limp, and I wondered what had happened.

The stories like the sands of the Gobi Desert were endless.

After a few days of writing, I started to cry, right there over my computer. I wanted to return to Mongolia to teach. Was I crazy" my ego shouted. *You're too old! What will others think?*

My mind was relentless like a dog with a bone.

I pulled up the school website. Days passed. I was afraid to say anything to anybody, but I was bursting inside with all the emotions one felt when confronted with a huge decision. My gut felt good, but still . . .

Putting aside my fears, I spoke with a few good friends. I was in search of much-needed counseling. There was no other way to say it, "I'm thinking of returning to Mongolia."

Their reactions were all the same: encouraging, not surprised, and supportive. But one lingering demon wouldn't let go: that experience that'd left a bad taste in my mouth— the teaching job in Indonesia. I was questioning myself, my judgment.

Another friend spoke up and said, "Stop right there, no one knew that would happen. You need to get back on the horse."

Did I hear it correctly? When I was younger, I used to ride, and one day I fell off the horse. I didn't remember if I was afraid to get back on (I was young and foolish), but the analogy hit home.

The fire that had started was slowly burning brighter. But still I gave it forty-eight hours. Finally I sat down and composed an email to the school, walked around the room before hitting the send button. The demons were in full force: what if they didn't want me? And worse, what if I never heard from them? Enough already, I hit the send button.

Within fifteen to twenty minutes I received a reply from the school's recruiter, "What a surprise to hear from you, and yes, we would love to have you return."

I jumped up and down, pumping the air with my fists like some kind of athlete; and yes, the tears flowed!

So I returned to Mongolia, to the same international school in the capital city of Ulaanbaatar where I had previously taught, but now I was going to teach second graders.

I was looking out once again toward the rolling hills that had always been so captivating and reassuring even though a little more lost with new apartment buildings that seemed to sprout up like weeds. But still on those same hills, I saw cows wandering in the snow, looking for food. And last night the full moon came up over those hills, first lighting up the sky with its eerie glow and then appearing as a round, bold ball in the Mongolian night sky.

It was more than a welcoming; I knew; it was an invitation to a life that I would discover held more promises than I could imagine.

I was well aware that changes had taken place in this seemingly idyllic setting, but change for the most part had never been my enemy. Someone once said that I knew how to reinvent myself better than anyone. A survivor, an eternal beginner.

As I thought back, most people who knew me were not surprised when I told them I was returning. They were genuinely excited for me, in awe that I would do this. But maybe not always aware at how I had struggled to get back on the horse? Demons were like that, never wanting to let go.

It sounded like a Cinderella story, but why not. Magic wasn't just left to the movies. Oh, the demons still reared their ugly heads! But when I listened to my heart, I knew I was where I should be, doing what I was doing.

CHAPTER 39

Returning to Mongolia

Dawa and I seemed to stay the same, while the other characters in the play changed. Some weaved in and out throughout your life, your stay, and others were only there for a brief moment, dropped in by another power perhaps.

My first time in Mongolia was like a first kiss, first falling in love, first time experimenting with sex, your firstborn—it was magic because it was new, untried, exciting. But also scary, frightening, with the unsure sense I might be beyond myself.

The second time was that feeling of having been tested and more than survived: flourished with a feeling of a conquering warrior who was home. I felt it in my bones, in my steps wherever my feet landed.

But even so, I knew things would be different. I had heard rumors, seen photos of the new addition to the school, which meant gers gone; and also more expensive apartment buildings intertwined with gers and people who lived with outhouses and no running water and burned everything from coal to trash. They merely wanted to keep their children warm and safe from the harsh cold. Who could blame them? We all thought about the kids, babies—teachers, parents, grandparents, extended families.

I was so excited about returning that I left early, the second week in August, to get a feel for the place once again. To be a part of something once again! It did not disappoint. I didn't have a fourth-floor apartment (not the princess in the tower), but instead on the second floor, still facing the hills, which were being overgrown with new, tall apartment buildings, but never the less the hills were alive, and the moon was as awesome as ever. I could have sung, *"The hills are alive!"*

Oh yes! In those three years, they had finished a huge apartment complex that blocked even more of the hills and sometimes the moon, but never completely. We welcomed each other back like old friends remembering.

But the goats were gone, taken over by progress. I always looked for the goats even after three years until my final day, and I looked for red pajama guy. The goat path was still there, but the apartments had blocked the path to their pens, which were probably also gone. But not to fear, in their place, at least occasionally, were the wandering cows and sometimes a herder.

It was enough. More than enough.

I really liked my studio apartment, which had been redone with a very nice kitchen countertop, lots of glass cabinets; still the Barbie stove with two electric burners. But who needs more? A bigger fridge and now Wi-Fi, and a better TV than I had at home: a flat screen. I got right to work, rearranging the furniture, and made it home for the next three years. There were four other apartments on my floor, and I met the couple next to me and the guy who was now in my old apartment. I had heard a couple was moving in across from me—later I would meet Steve and Christy, Christy became my second-grade teaching partner as well as a very dear friend for life.

It was fun seeing old faces like Roger who was now ES principal and his wife, Glenda, and of course, Oyuuna, the owner of the school.

I hurried to get set up my weekly shopping spree with Dawa. It was so great to hear his voice again. And that he remembered me. And seeing him was even better.

I also called my former assistant, Boogii, and when she came to my apartment, we hugged and cried like we did when I left three years before. I met her husband and her sweet little son, Khuchit. We, of course, went down to Cozy Nomads as we reminisced about old times. She wasn't going to be my assistant; she had gotten a really great job at another school. But I would have Muugii from those first years, and how lucky I was.

I couldn't believe all the changes in Zaisan, new stores, new restaurants. I was happy, but also sad for the loss of what had once been—one restaurant and one market—remembering walking that first day in 2009 with Mr. Chris. But progress was knocking on the door. It seemed it had a plan even in Mongolia.

My first stop was Millie's, and seeing the owner, Daniel, who also remembered me even though my hair was now white. Hugs all around. I ordered my favorite: café mocha, scrambled eggs with bacon and toast.

I was back! I could have sung the song from *Cheers*.

On the first Saturday after meeting Christy, Steve, and Morene, the third-grade teacher, I played travel agent and took them all around downtown UB. First stop was Millie's and then, of course, Chinggis Khan Square, or CK as we called it (formally Sukhbaatar Square). It was fun seeing it through the eyes of newbies and being the "expert." Who would have thought?

The old standby places were still around, but new places had been added. Coffee Bean and Tea Leaf. Really? Amsterdam Café was still there—the expat and backpacker hangout.

Back at school, elementary was now in the new building, and MS and HS were in the old building. I guess I was a creature of habit because I missed my old classroom down in the "cellar" of the old building, but I tried to embrace the new. More technology. I always said I wasn't a techy person, but I relied on others like Christy and was bound and determined to learn, and I did.

Christy and I hit it off right away and remained friends even after she and Steve left for China on a new assignment, and I stayed on in Mongolia for another year. We met in Hong Kong for her fortieth birthday.

She, like my friend Chris, and I shared many adventures. We loved getting pedicures at the place right down the road from our apartment, then going next door to treat ourselves to the best French fries and a glass of red wine. One particular late afternoon, I was getting my pedicure. The pedicurists liked to scrape off the dead skin, and there was a lot of dead skin because of the cold and very dry weather. I guess I wasn't paying attention, because all of a sudden I saw blood in the basin. At first I didn't panic, but when it wouldn't stop, and they couldn't stop it, I started to panic. They started to panic. Everyone was running around and talking fast with that deer-in-the-headlights look.

Finally I called Christy who brought a ton of bandages. She applied pressure and (I was sure) waved a magic wand, because the bleeding stopped. The pedicurists couldn't apologize enough! I hobbled next door with Christy who called a taxi. While we waited, we had those delicious fries and yes! A glass of wine!

We shared Dawa with our once-a-week shopping on Tuesdays. We got it down to a science by leaving at 4:15, two stores and home in less than one hour. We found a store like Costco, right down to the roasting chickens. Apparently, the owner of Nomin's Warehouse in UB had been to the States, saw Costco, and set about to duplicate the store. My treat to myself for grocery shopping day was sushi and a beer from Good Price, the upscale, Western-type market. Oh! And those delicious, chewy chocolates.

And we only had to shlep up to the second floor.

Life was good!

I had my favorite places to explore, but I really loved the Art Museum, which was near the Square and hidden. Very few people were ever in there so I could explore all the paintings and artifacts in quiet. After working with second graders all week, I needed the quiet. But one day I came across an art class for young children in the backroom. No one spoke English and they were as curious about me as I was about them. Mongolian parents made sure their children were exposed to all the arts, including playing the violin and piano.

A Saturday would find me at Millie's in the morning and if not, the Art Museum, then the ger monastery where occasionally I got to see a Buddhist ceremony. I loved seeing the Buddhists in their orange/red robes, walking around town. I missed that. If I really felt special, I might end up at the Shangri-La Hotel for tea and late lunch with wine perhaps, then a taxi home.

People at home wondered what I did in Mongolia. But I found that I had more to explore than at home. Worlds to conquer.

They said *you can't go home again*, and I suppose there is some truth to that. But even though a lot had changed in UB, Zaisan, and at the school, I embraced the change, looking for ways to make it work for me. I took on each challenge, finding my own success. After all, change was never my enemy. And remember, I was "home."

CHAPTER 40

Restaurants

I was not a foodie . . . well, except for the times I went to Italy. How could anyone not be a foodie there? I like food and I definitely want a good meal and to enjoy the local cuisine; but for me, eating out was about being with friends and/or getting to know the people in the restaurant, coffeehouse, etc. It was about relationships.

I liked the comedy, *Frasier*, and there was an episode where Frasier and his brother Niles thought they would have to leave their favorite coffee shop and referred to it as their Chez Away From Chez (home away from home), and how important it was for them to have that place/connection.

Bingo! Even now that I was back home in Southern California, I looked for places that could give me a Chez Away From Chez experience. That Starbucks feeling, but so much more. More like my Tom N Toms experience from one of my favorite coffee places in Zaisan, not far from my apartment.

Restaurants were different the second time I came to Mongolia—more of the upscale Western type, but for the most part still run by Mongolians. And very eclectic Indian, Korean, Italian, Western steak places. My favorite Mongolian food was *buuz*, the dumpling filled with beef, pork (sometimes only mutton) and cabbage. Although some cooks did a better job making it moist and tender, like my assistant, Muugii.

The first year I arrived, I discovered Cozy Nomads right down the street from school, a sort of upscale family restaurant also selling upscale decorating items for the home—mostly from other places, some from Mongolia. If the weather was good in fall and spring, I walked down there and then stopped at Rosie's Market to pick up a few items. However, when desperate even in the freezing cold with ice everywhere, I walked there and took a taxi back. I had lunch or dinner with a glass of wine or just a coffee with something sweet and hopefully get the table by the window and watch the world go by.

Whether it was the cows wandering, and/or the young Mongolians all bundled up, if it was still cold, coming from up above where they lived close to Bogd Khan and catching buses to town. Especially that first year I went there alone on Sunday afternoon and sometimes another teacher was there and we nodded to each other, an unspoken message that this was our alone time away from all. I got to know the owners, especially the woman who had traveled numerous times to America.

Many Friday afternoons after school, Chris and I walked to Cozy and ordered the raspberry dish with a glass of red wine. My first experience with wine in UB at any restaurant was a short pour and a little expensive. Most of the restaurants got better as the years went on, more wine, but the same price.

Amsterdam Café, right on the main drag, not too far from State Department Store, and written up in travel guides, was a great place to find expats. Also a great place to check out the backpackers making their way across Asia with UB and the Gobi Desert on their checklist. It was where I met Ayush, the old Mongolian painter, who was doing six oils for me for Christmas gifts for friends and family: one of me and my grandson that I still cherish. I bought a pencil drawing from him of a little Mongolian girl out in the countryside, holding a goat. For me it represented all of what and who Mongolia is.

Another hangout was a café across from State Department that reminded me of Starbucks, but better. A little coffeehouse across from the Meditation Center was always quiet. In 2014, I discovered the River Grande near the Tuul River in Zaisan and if the weather was nice I sat outside and watched the river flow.

When I first arrived in 2009, State Department Store was the only Nordstrom-type store, but a far cry from Nordy! It was one of the old Soviet buildings and outside on the top were the dates in big numbers: 1989–2009, Mongolia became its own sovereign country and no longer a satellite of Russia in 1989. It had six floors and even a supermarket. Suffice to say, it was a tourist attraction in itself. It was one of our hangouts, and when I came back in 2014, the Mongolians had built a couple of malls and a store that almost looked like Nordstrom.

Georgetown and UBean were new places in 2014. I enjoyed many Sunday afternoon lunches at Georgetown on the upper floor by the window, watching dogs roam the area, or the cars on the river ice. I found a quiet corner, ordered hamburger with fries, a glass of wine, sometimes dessert, but always an extra-hot cappuccino while I continued to take in the river with its surrounding activities.

UBean sat on the river and I passed the time relaxing after wandering the city on a Saturday going to my art museums or Buddhist monasteries and enjoyed a coffee drink.

In 2011 after two years, my last meal out before departing to come home was at Cozy Nomads with Chris with a glass of red wine.

In 2017, my last meal was at Millie's, just me saying goodbye. And always the breakfast.

CHAPTER 41

$700 Water Bill

I owned a condo in Southern California that I didn't rent out while I was in Mongolia. It sat empty, much to my accountant's ire. But in five years, I was lucky and had only one sort of near disaster. For the first two years, my close neighbor checked on it, took in the mail, got rid of all those annoying flyers hanging off the patio chairs, started the car. For the other three years, my son took over.

When I came home in summer 2016, a notice on my garage door said that the condo association needed to fix the water pipes—a repipe. This all needed to be done in September while I would be teaching in UB. Fortunately, I was greeted by another great neighbor who said he would help me out by giving them access to my condo, taking care of my car and any other issues. Wonderful! How lucky was I!

Before I went back to Mongolia at the end of the summer, I had prepared my house by putting away all breakables, talked with the powers that be, and gave all my keys to home and car to my wonderful neighbor. Work was starting in September and would be done in four days. Very fast! After it was done, I checked with everyone, and all seemed to be fine. Then one day as I was checking my emails for bills, etc., I noticed that I had a $700.00 water bill—usually it was around $45.00. Needless to say, I panicked. Somehow I contacted my nephew to get in touch with my neighbor. Not easy with a fifteen to sixteen-hour time difference. But thank God for technology.

You got it . . . my fear was that I had a water leak in the house, and the condo would be a mess! As it turned out, the repipe company had stepped on my sprinkler system, breaking off pieces, and caused the water to not turn off. Fortunately for me, the water company had come out, noticed the meter running amuck, and shut off the sprinklers. But I was still responsible for, *ouch*, $700.00. The repipe company never took any responsibility! Claiming, "Not our responsibility." *Ugh!*

I believed in karma.

CHAPTER 42

Camel and the Post Office

Chris and I went into town early because we wanted to go to Mary & Martha's before heading to our Indian restaurant. Mary & Martha's was owned by Scottish expats who came to Mongolia some ten years ago and, in their words, "We were just going to stay for a short time, but here we are some ten years later!"

You could buy every souvenir possible, all handmade: bags, clothing, footwear, cards, home décor . . . the list went on. But what I liked about the store was they supported women artisans throughout Mongolia. Many women from the countryside, from the city. It became a stomping ground for me. Buying unique gifts to take home. Book marks made of bone and horse's hair was easy to stuff in my suitcase.

Other items I shipped home, well, I tried to ship home.

There was only one post office in UB, a large Soviet-type block building. This day I had bought some gifts including a small, felt Bactrian camel for my little grandson. All to be shipped. I was ready to walk down to the post office when the owner stopped me and said, "Let me walk you down, and I'll show you what you need to do to ship this home."

I probably looked at him funny, but then realized he knew what he was talking about, so off we went with bags and whatnot.

When it was all said and done, I swore there were six steps to the process, at least. The most important was to not seal the package until a postal worker had a chance to look inside and make sure you were sending what you said you were sending. Everything had to match, and it was imperative to follow the steps in order. Finally, done and off went the packages, including the camel back to California.

I was never quite sure what happened to the camel, but apparently our post office back home tried to deliver it, signature required, and that had never happened, so it was shipped back from California to Ulaanbaatar, Mongolia. One day at school I got a notice saying I needed to pick up a package from the post office. I didn't have a clue; thought someone was sending me something. How exciting!

But alas! There was the camel. Many weeks later. I kept the camel as a mascot for my first graders, and we named it after my grandson. The camel that traveled the Pacific Ocean twice over 12,000 miles. When I left UB, I gave it to one of my students, who was thrilled to have such a prestigious gift.

CHAPTER 43

Reflection

Mongolia opened my eyes to a different adventure, one that changed my life forever and continues to touch me even today. It took me from only being a traveler who barely tasted the land to one who became a part of the land, a part of the people, a part of the culture. So that when I travel now, I am almost unconsciously looking for that deeper meaning. Not merely what the land can give me, but what I can give back. What about the people who live there? Whether I lived in one of the coldest capitals in the world or on a remote, tropical island, I was aware of a deeper meaning, the importance of family, culture. The importance of connecting.

Mongolia caused me to question myself, my values. I had read about others having the same experience, as if the very earth of Mongolia, the desert, the mountains, the lakes, was in our bones, in our marrow, in our blood. It was almost like I had no choice, but in a good way. If a place could beckon you, then this place beckoned me. With Chinggis Khan becoming a part of me . . . and me him.

My North Star.

The people I met who were not Mongolian have ended up in the four corners of the earth. But we all seem connected by this magical place and experience. We remember the faces of the old, the smooth faces of the young, the faces of the curious. The eyes.

All imprinted on us like footprints in the sand.

Time was an enemy as it causes us to forget—and I didn't want to forget. I wanted to continue to go to places that felt like the ends of the earth. To care.

To have the eagle within me.

As Thoreau said in Walden, "I went to the woods because I wished to live deliberately, to front only the essential facts of life, and see if I could not learn what it had to teach, and not, when I came to die, discover that I had not lived."

About The Author

Diane Height's writing and photography are inspired by her love of travel, adventure, and the world at large. She was an elementary teacher in Southern California before embarking on her own odyssey, teaching for five years at an international school in Ulaanbaatar, Mongolia. She has also taught in Indonesia, Cambodia, and Italy. Her short stories have appeared in various publications. This is her first book. To learn more about her adventures in the land of the eternal blue sky as well as discovering the warmth of the Mongolian people, please visit her blog: http://dianeheight-thewanderingnomad.blogspot.com/

Made in USA - North Chelmsford, MA
1349521_9798987419205
12.28.2022 1149